# Anselm Kiefer

# Anselm Kiefer
# The Psychology of "After the Catastrophe"

Rafael López-Pedraza

For Jutta
from
Amasa
6.03

George Braziller New York

Simultaneously published in 1996 in the United States by George Braziller, Inc.,
in the United Kingdom by Thames and Hudson, Ltd., and in Venezuela by Editorial Arte.



For information, please address the publisher:
George Braziller, Inc.
171 Madison Avenue
New York, NY 10016

Library of Congress Cataloging-in-Publication Data:

López-Pedraza, Rafael, 1920–
Anselm Kiefer : the psychology of "after the catastrophe" / Rafael López-Pedraza.
p. cm.
Includes bibliographical references.
ISBN 0-8076-1415-7
1. Kiefer, Anselm, 1945—Psychology. 2. Jung, C. G. (Carl Gustav), 1875-1961—Influence. 1. Title.
ND588.K464L66 1996
759.3—dc20 96-9026
CIP



Designer: Gisela Viloria
Coordinator: Robert Violette, London
Set in Garamond
Printed by Editorial Arte, Caracas, Venezuela

First Edition 1996

# ACKNOWLEDGMENTS

I would like to give special thanks to my old friend Niel Micklem for his cogent reading of the images of *Parsifal* and *Zweistromland*.

With many thanks to Teresa Berbín and Iván Rodríguez del Camino for their invaluable collaboration in the preparation of the text, and to Ruth Horine for her translation of Peter-Klaus Schuster's "Saturn, Melancholie und Merkur"; to Juan Bofill, Rafael Cadenas, Mercedes Carrillo Gil, Sarah Janson, Marina López Pedraza, Eduardo Machado Iturbe, Mariela Provenzali and Marco Rodríguez del Camino, who in different ways have been of great help in making this book possible.

My gratitude to Luis Miguel La Corte of Editorial Arte for his understanding and support throughout the production of this book. And I extend warm thanks to Anthony d'Offay and Lorcan O'Neill of the Anthony d'Offay Gallery, London, for all their cooperation and interest in my work, and for permission to quote from *The High Priestess;* to Mark Rosenthal for permission to quote from his catalogue *Anselm Kiefer*, 1987, and to Peter-Klaus Schuster to quote from his essay "Saturn, Melancholie und Merkur: Bemerkungen zu Kiefers 'Saturnischer Malkunst.'"

And last but not least I would like to express my gratitude to Anselm Kiefer for his generous collaboration and for supplying the illustrations.

*To my wife, Valerie*

# THE PSYCHOLOGY OF "AFTER THE CATASTROPHE"

Anselm Kiefer, the German painter, was born in the town of Donaueschingen at the source of the Danube in 1945, the year that saw the end of World War II. In the same year, C. G. Jung wrote an essay, "After the Catastrophe," which I have taken for the subtitle of this book.

Of all the volumes comprising C. G. Jung's *Collected Works,* that called *Civilization in Transition* (vol. 10) differs considerably from the others in that it contains the three essays in which Jung reflects, dramatically, Western culture's tragedy of Hitler, National Socialism, and World War II. They are published as *Essays on Contemporary Events*, a work that marks the first time a great psychiatrist addresses a historical catastrophe with his own psychiatric view.

In "Wotan" (CW10: 371), the first of these essays, written in 1936, Jung forecasts the coming "storm" and presents an unprecedented psychological picture of the German people, based on their mythology. Almost with the precision of a diagnosis, he brings a psycho-biological view, which demonstrates that the characteristics of the German god Wotan go a long way toward explaining the historical behavior of the Germans in terms of a particular biology. Jung (CW10: 375, 389) describes him as "the god of storm and frenzy, the unleasher of passions and the lust of battle" and also as "a fundamental attribute of the German psyche":

> As an autonomous psychic factor, Wotan produces effects in the collective life of a people and thereby reveals his own nature. For Wotan has a peculiar biology of his own, quite apart from the nature of man (CW10: 391).

Undoubtedly the psychology of the Germans

was a challenge for Jung, an inborn challenge for a Swiss, who speaks a German dialect and yet is ethnically different from the Germans living as close neighbors just across the Rhine. It was probably this challenge that led him to the acute observation of the Wotanic trait in the German people at the biological level. We know about Jung's lifelong struggle to reconcile the opposition between psychology and science. It would seem that in his essay "Wotan" he freed himself from this conflict. In using the scientific term "biology" to describe a factor in the German psyche that leads to a state of possession, madness and destruction, and in attributing it to the god Wotan rather than directly to human nature, we can say he was using the term metaphorically. In this way, Jung freed the imagination from the strictures of scientific "proof."

One feature of German mythology stands out strongly. When compared to a more highly differentiated mythology, such as that of the Greeks, it is clear that where certain traits are carried by one god, they would in Greek mythology be distributed among several divinities, each with its own archetypal realm. According to comparative mythology, German mythology displays a lack of differentiation between gods and heroes, and therefore creates psychic confusion. It is essentially a mythology of warriors—both gods and heroes—and there is a strong emphasis on heroic death. The German sense of destiny is not accompanied by a tragic emotional reflection of life, as for example is the Greek, but is related to that heroic death. Jung conveys the volatile danger inherent in such a mythology, a mythology that may catch one from behind and move quickly into identification and madness, a mythology that leads to sudden states of possession.

Other European nations have also displayed a strong Wotanic unconscious but these, through the long historical process of assimilating the influence of Christianity and other cultures, have managed to transform the powerful forces Wotan unleashes. These nations seem to have succeeded in defusing the collective danger. They have become settings wherein the individual may remain more conscious and less vulnerable to identification with unconscious Wotanic forces. Wotanic German mythology gives a picture of a powerful irrationality, and the repetitive manifestations of this mythological complex suggest an extreme autonomy and a form of suffering that seems to be at the core of the German people's fate. Could it be that this Wotanic biological factor, referred to by Jung, gives to the German people their ethnic characteristics? In this first essay, Jung presents a pathography of the Germans in which one sees the unique ways their nature and history are so closely related. Their historical fate is an expression of their nature.

Jung begins his second essay, "After the Catastrophe," written in 1945, with these words:

> This is the first time since 1936 that the fate of Germany again drives me to take up my pen. The quotation from the Volupso with which I ended the article I wrote at that time, about Wotan "murmuring with Mimir's head," pointed prophetically to the nature of the coming apocalyptic events. The myth has been fulfilled, and the greater part of Europe lies in ruins (CW10: 400).

Jung's first reaction was a call "above all for reflection. Questions are being asked on all sides about the meaning of the tragedy" (CW10: 401). In his search for meaning, what Jung found first of all was "collective guilt." He explains:

> The psychological use of the word "guilt" should not be confused with guilt in the legal or moral sense. Psychologically, it connotes the irrational presence of a subjective feeling (or conviction) of guilt, or an objective imputation of, or imputed share in, guilt (CW10: 403).

For Jung, the feeling of "after the catastrophe" was one of collective guilt. In this essay, he conveys all the outrage of a great European at the apocalyptic proportions of the destructiveness of the German madness. His use of the word "apocalyptic" stresses the devastation and the collapse of the current values of Western culture. We feel all his shame, anger, and guilt in front of this failure of Western civilization. It is a challenging treatise on collective guilt in which he states: "Psychological collective guilt is a tragic fate," and he emphasizes that it was not the German guilt alone, but the guilt of Europe as a whole (CW10: 405).

Jung also tackles evil: "When evil breaks out at any point into the order of things, our whole circle of psychic protection is disrupted" (CW10: 411). These words tell us a great deal about the psychological impact of the catastrophe and the destruction of the values of that order the psyche was unable to protect. He then goes on to introduce the term *pseudologia phantastica*, referring to Hitler, "that form of hysteria which is characterized by a peculiar talent for believing one's own lies" (CW10: 419).

Later, he explains:

> the "hysterical" disposition forms a sub-division of what are known as "psychopathic inferiorities." This term by no means implies that the individual or the nation is "inferior" in every respect, but only that there is a place of least resistance, a peculiar instability, which exists independently of all other qualities (CW10: 423).

Jung explains the psychological reality at the base of this peculiar state of hysteria in which a leader and a nation are charismatically bound together. We can speculate, here, about a strange region in human nature where psychopathic inferiority resides and which, when activated, produces the most blind and destructive state of possession—possession by evil. This would be a region where the soul does not work. It could be said to be the place of the "soulless beings" of colloquial tradition.

In the essay "Wotan," Jung brings a picture of the German people that we can associate with a collective psychosis, a state of possession by a god. In "After the Catastrophe," written just after World War II, he complements the previous diagnosis with a psychiatric view of the psychopathic components at work in the catastrophe. In "The Fight with the Shadow," the third essay written in 1946, Jung deals with a specific "shadow" rooted in German biology.[1] The three *Essays on Contemporary Events*, taken together, form a basic text that is indispensable for learning about the human shadow in its darkest and most collective manifestation.

Jung was very specific as to the shadow that had to be fought:

> Like the rest of the world, they [the Germans] did not understand wherein Hitler's significance lay, that he symbolized something in every individual. He was the most prodigious personification of all human inferiorities. He was an utterly incapable, unadapted, irresponsible, psychopathic personality, full of empty, infantile fantasies, but cursed with the keen intuition of a rat or a guttersnipe. He represented the shadow, the inferior part of everybody's personality, in an overwhelming degree, and this was another reason why they fell for him (CW10: 454).

Earlier, Jung described the leader as "found in the individual who has the least resistance, the least sense of responsibility and, because of his inferiority, the greatest will to power" (CW10: 449). Here, Jung explains the psychological mechanism at work in the mystery of man's drive for power. So we are confronted with the shadow of power, the most challenging shadow of all:

> But what could they have done? In Hitler, every German should have seen his own shadow, his own worst danger. It is everybody's allotted fate to become conscious of and learn to deal with this shadow. But how could the Germans be expected to understand this, when nobody in the world can understand such a simple truth? The world will never reach a state of order until this truth is generally recognized (CW10: 455).

The above reflection on the shadow of power was written in relation to Hitler, nonetheless it has a historical dimension, for a new consciousness is still demanded for studying the appearance of power. It is as if Jung raised the curtain onto a new act on the stage of history, and I like to imagine that it is Anselm Kiefer who is now in charge of the scenography of this act.

We can now see that the drive for power, the consequence of this shadow of inferiority, is evil. These complexities of power and evil, so rooted in human nature, and the producers of such a huge German historical complex, seem to haunt Anselm Kiefer, impelling him to fight this terrible shadow with the one weapon he has: his creative art.

There is the urgent need to fight the shadow and to reflect on the madness in history. Jung helps us in this respect; Anselm Kiefer, with the emotional impact of his art, deepens our reflection on the catastrophe itself and, more importantly, on the psychology of "after the catastrophe." He inaugurates a new way of reflecting man's most destructive shadow. And his furthering of Jung's reflections supports my theory that psychology learns from art.

Now, after this brief preparatory reflection on Jung's three essays, we can turn to Kiefer's work. To introduce Kiefer, a painter, as being able to broaden the insights and knowledge of a psychologist perhaps has no antecedents. But there is no option other than to surrender to the evidence: words may get entangled in semantics, but an image speaks directly to the emotions.

Anselm Kiefer seems to be representative of a new generation of German artists who are painfully aware of the terrible history they have inherited. Kiefer reflects the suffering brought about by the pressure of the German complexes and brings a historical perspective not only to his own tragedy, but also to that of his country and Western culture. Kiefer's work, like Jung's essays, offers vivid examples for studying the mythological and historical background of the German people.

My approach in this study will be to explore, drawing from my years of practice as a Jungian psychotherapist and my interest in art, the personality of Kiefer himself and his creativity. He has demonstrated that he has a strong enough psyche to activate in himself the German past, its mythology, and history from its primitive beginnings to Hitler and National Socialism. Through a retrograde movement of the psyche, he reaches a symmetry with the contents he pursues. Kiefer mobilizes his imaginative creativity by way of a regression into the historical past.[2] I contend that we must view such a regression in the Jungian sense, namely, as a search for oneself. In the case of Kiefer, part of the search for himself is through Germany's historical past and its collective unconscious, within himself.

It seems that Kiefer is very gifted in finding different ways to stimulate his creativity through psychic regression. We shall consider some of these regressive movements. Kiefer belongs to a post-war generation of German artists who like to express their art *in vivo*. In 1969, as a young art student of twenty-four, Kiefer traveled extensively in Europe, "occupying" various locations:

> He visited places with more or less historic implications—among them Küssnacht and Bellinzona, then Rome, Paestum, and Pompeii, as well as Montpellier, Arles, and Sête, in order to pose there, in empty spaces, with "his arm raised in the Hitler salute" (Adriani, 1991: 13–14).

We can imagine the young Kiefer, traveling around Europe, taking his photographs in a state of exaltation, playing out Hitler's demented

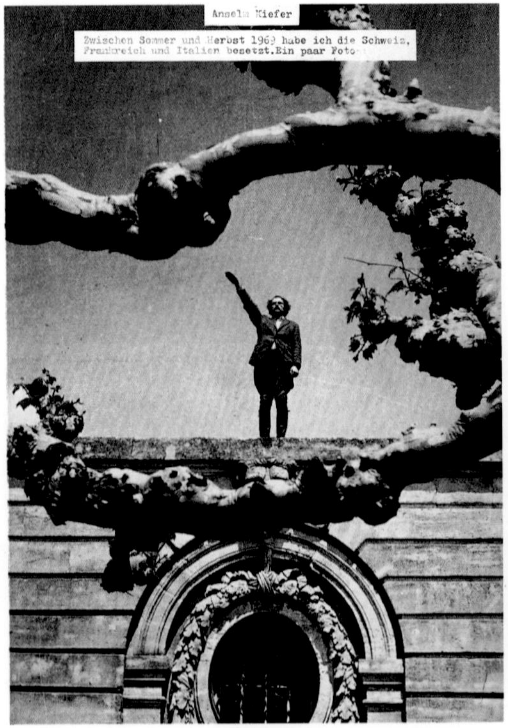


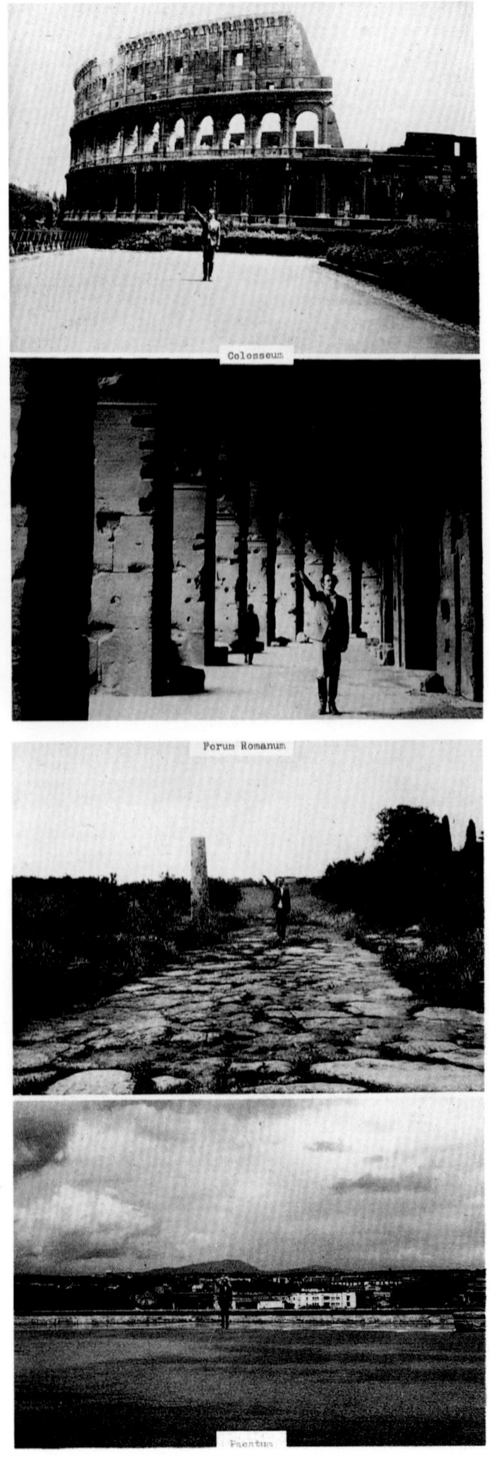


**Occupations,** 1975

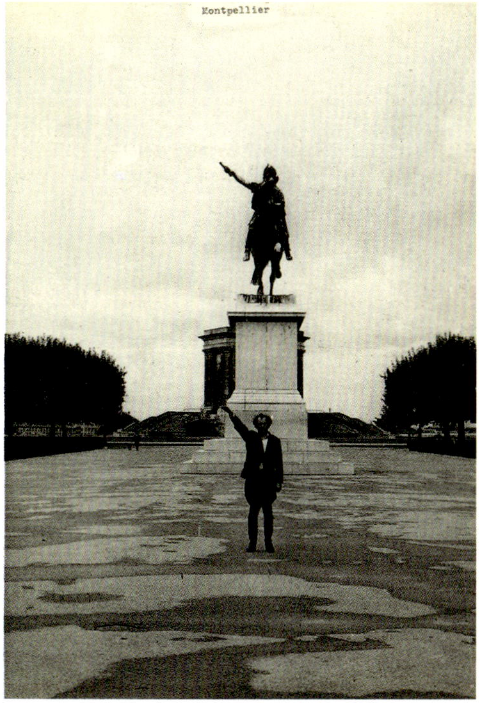


Occupations, 1975

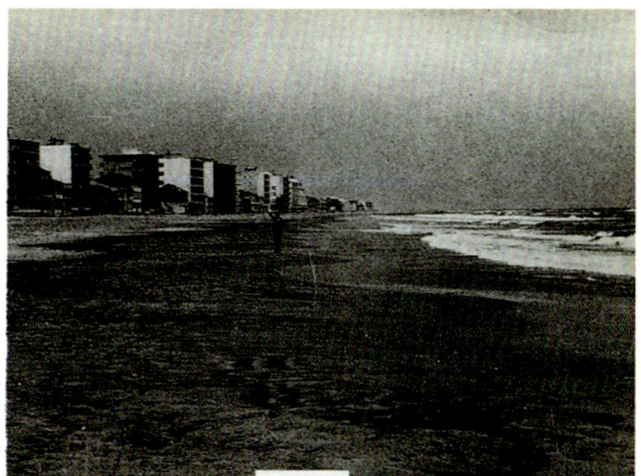

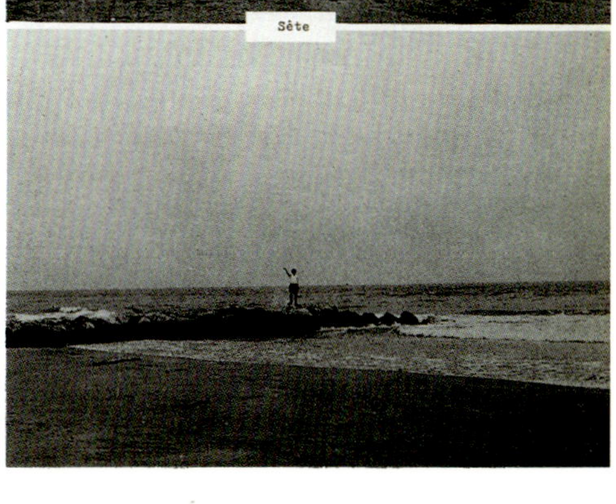


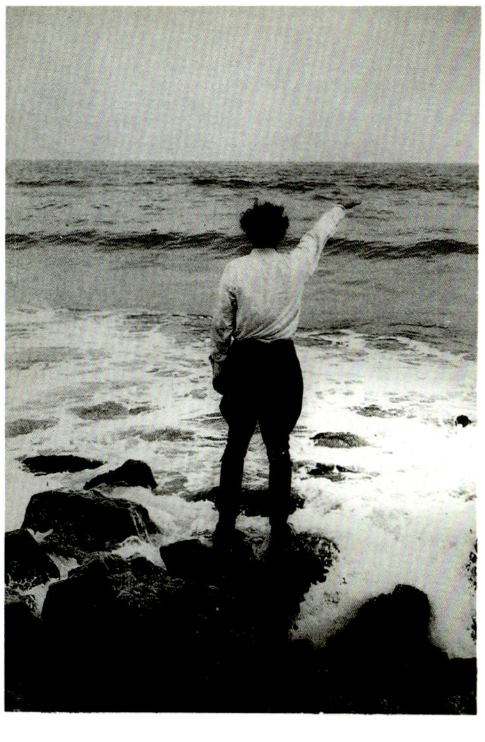

fantasy of dominating the whole of Europe (pages 14–15). "His intention was to integrate the taboo subjects, until then stored carefully in a sort of collective forgetfulness, into the artistic process" (Adriani, 1991: 14). From the beginning, Kiefer was deeply aware of the importance of what he was doing, both for Germany's historical memory and for the processes of artistic creativity. This series of photographs, called Occupations (see Rosenthal, 1987: 15), received a negative response when first exhibited in Germany.

> The negative points of the photographic sequences —which, by the way, were the subject of Kiefer's examination at the Karlsruhe Academy and were defended in the face of the professors by Peter Dreyer, his longtime teacher, and by Rainer Kuchenmeister, a former concentration camp inmate —make clear nothing more than the sarcasm of a young artist directing his questions toward a pernicious iconography (Adriani, 1991: 14).

This passage gives us an idea of the atmosphere prevailing in Germany during the late 1960s. Evidently the new generation of artists were desperately looking for new ways of expression in accordance with the German reality of "after the catastrophe." In the catalogue *Anselm Kiefer*, Mark Rosenthal mentions the late 1960s conceptualist movement, and that Kiefer's photographic "staged tableaux recall, too, the manifestations of performance art and happenings of that period" (1987: 17). Through the magic art of an action, he "occupied" various locations in Europe by making the most stereotyped sign of Nazism—the Sieg Heil—and in so doing he became psychologically symmetric with the Nazi past and, at the same time, carried the Nazi salute into a field of deep reflection. Undoubtedly, Rosenthal saw the further importance of these photos when he said: "'Occupations' signaled the direction Kiefer's work would take in the following decade: he endeavored to use his vocation to explore his own identity and heritage" (Ibid.).

After considering the generational aspect, my own interest in Occupations is the artistic breakthrough it displays and its psychology of the body in action. Kiefer himself explained the psychology behind this sort of gesture: "I do not identify with Nero or Hitler, but I have to reenact what they did just a little bit in order to understand their madness" (Ibid.). One sees here a very original approach: as well as making a psychological regression to the German past, specifically to National Socialism, he is borrowing from the actor's technique and reenacting the role of Hitler. He is contained and protected in this personification by Dionysus, the god of theater and, paradoxically, of madness. We can view the figure in these photographs as an actor making an acquaintance with evil through the technique of his acting, and challenging the viewer to contemplate the implications.

The evil in Nazism is usually viewed in terms of

the opposites good and evil, a view which does not promote any deep understanding of this force; on the contrary, it only constellates the madness of a new Manicheanism. Kiefer's symmetric approach to Nazism paves the way for a different understanding through an awareness of the madness personified by the Nazi. Both Jung and Kiefer convey to us that consciousness of evil is no longer the prerogative of religion or the law: today, evil requires an effort of awareness and reflection. Kiefer's search for new ways to reflect evil deserves all the recognition we can give to it. In these photographs, by way of a gesture that synthesizes a painful history, he depicts a living psychology stemming from that shadow. It seems to me that Kiefer is not at the mercy of preconceived systems and so brings a bolder and more psychic approach to the issue.

Another impression of Occupations is that the photographs have a histrionic or hysterical character. This effect comes in part from the enthusiasm of Kiefer's generation for art performance or "happenings" which, as already mentioned, was a historical need to break through the barriers of worn-out forms in order to find new expression. Whereas other artists of his generation might present their art performances and actions in a very intellectual or personal way, as a sort of autobiographical narrative, Kiefer tells the whole story of Hitler and National Socialism through an economy of gesture, by making the very commonplace Nazi salute. He accepts and makes capital of the compulsive repetition that characterized the Nazi salute, and I believe in this way he challenges psychology, especially a psychology interested in "reading" the body as an image. Here again we are in the realm of Dionysus, knowing that Dionysus is always the body.

Kiefer's insistence on this repetitive compulsive element—the endless, inflated Sieg Heil—allowed him to take boredom ad infinitum. It also led him to other conceptions. In his book *Heroic Symbols*, 1969, he displays a deeply moving series of photographs and watercolors on the same theme. In two of the watercolors (page 18), we see a rather poor specimen of a man giving the Nazi salute in front of a body of water. These paintings transmit a different feeling to that of the ironic and sarcastic Occupations. The figure of this poor little man reveals the demise of the horrifying inflation of the Nazi millennium—the "Thousand Year Reich"—and conveys a new consciousness concerning National Socialism. In an indirect way, Kiefer leads us into considering a millennium in which humankind would have had to make the Nazi salute incessantly and compulsively; in so doing he touches a psychology that has not been explored: that of an unparalleled dementia. It is with a soul well-rooted in his body that Kiefer is able to explore such a madness.

In another book of his prolific production,

**Heroic Symbols**
1969

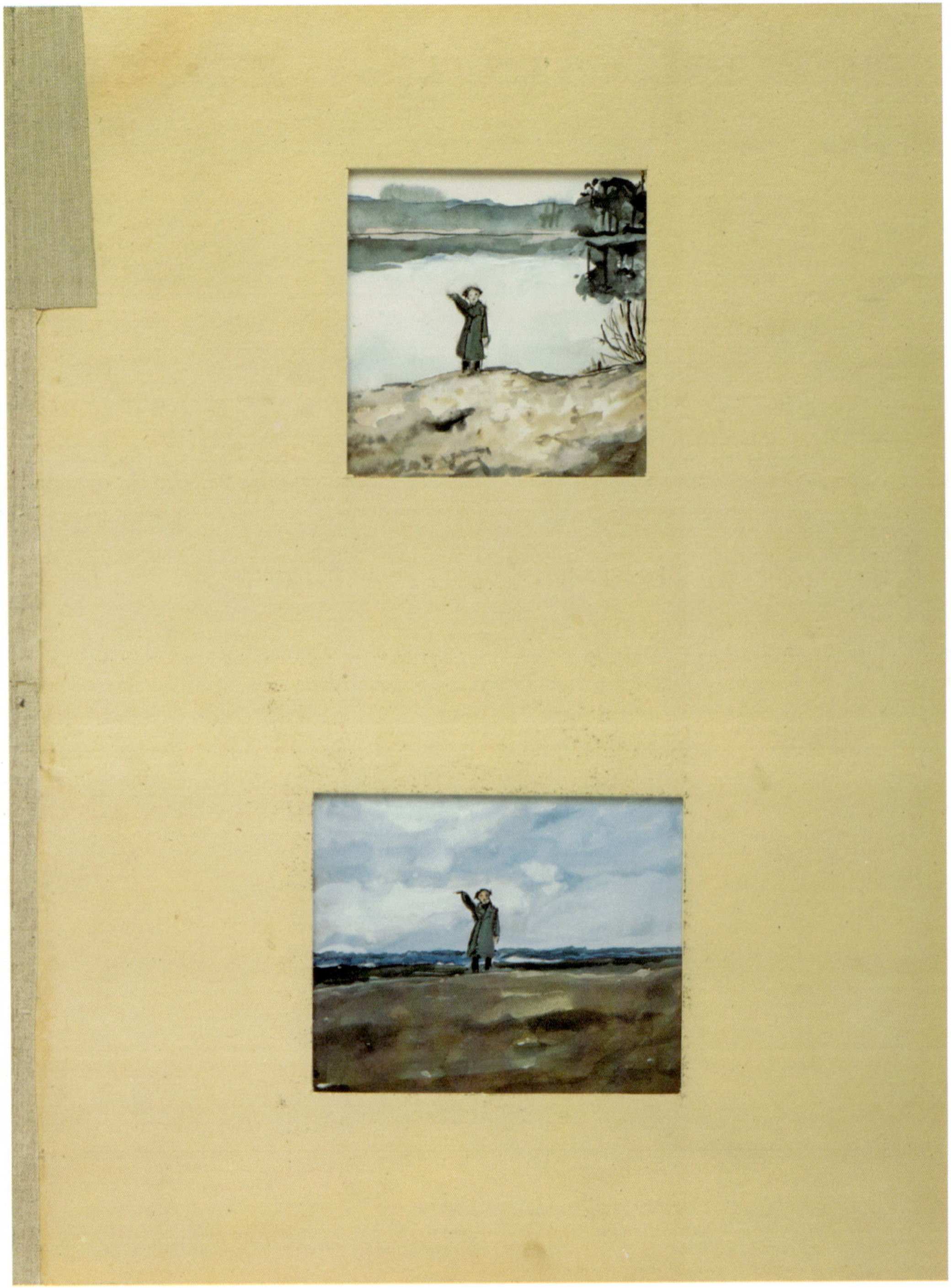

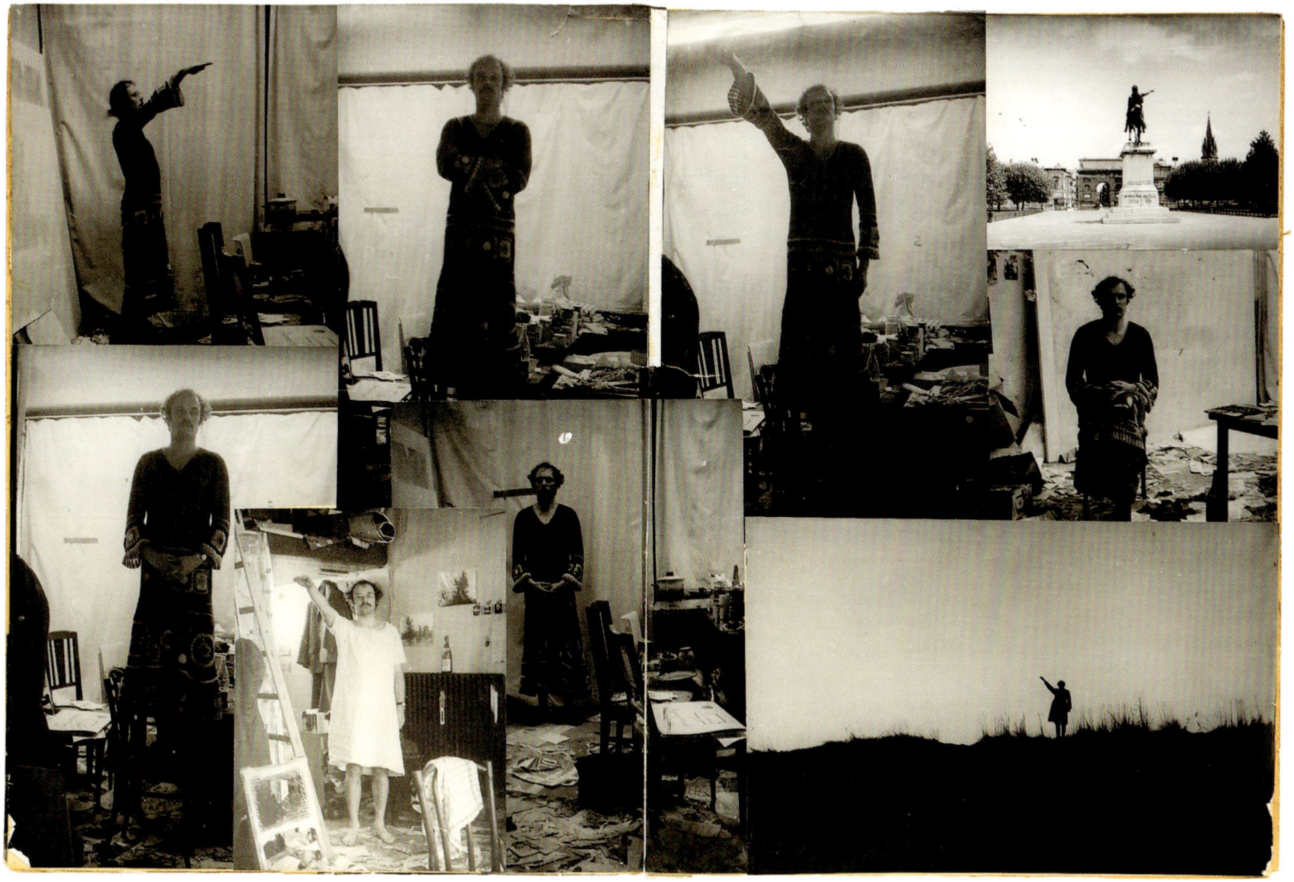

**To Genet**
1969

*To Genet,* 1969, he continues with the same theme. Here we see Kiefer, in odd garments and in more intimate and introverted settings, pondering the situation and making his Nazi salute, and we begin to see that the business of the salute is really no joke at all. As we look at Kiefer's photographic image, we become aware that, in activating the Nazi past in himself, he is indeed playing a risky game and, what is more, a depressing one. In these photographs, Kiefer reveals how difficult and painful it seems to have been for him, at this point, to move his body into making the salute. His very original way of living out or enacting his art has a great significance, as I have the impression that he is an introverted personality with a consciousness immersed in depression. He exposes himself within a precise limitation that strengthens the image, and undoubtedly this is his way of brooding on and ripening his psychological creative processes.

One begins to appreciate the tremendous concentration Kiefer has put into reflecting the Nazi salute. At the beginning of the book, we registered Jung's outrage and guilt in "After the Catastrophe," now, in this last series of photographs in *To Genet,* we register the emotion of shame in the expression of Kiefer's body. He brings us a living self-portrait, conveying an essential emotion for connecting to the Nazi past, and it is a level of connection felt in the body. The most characteristic psychology shared by Jung and Kiefer is the symmetric approach they brought to Nazism. Both felt the need to come close to the madness of Nazism in order to have an insight into its genesis. In the essay "Wotan," Jung wrote about the mythological roots of this German madness. And Kiefer, too, in his own very original way, gets in touch with these roots. Only through engaging in psychological symmetry could they have produced two such great achievements.

A number of Kiefer's large paintings support my thesis that psychology can be learned from art. Let us consider, first, *Operation Sea Lion I.* Operation Sea Lion was the code name for the German plan to invade Britain during World War II. It is well known that the German high command used to work out their strategy for the operation with toy boats in a water tank. Before tackling *Operation Sea Lion I,* Kiefer worked with the idea by playing with little toy boats in a bathtub, and under the spell of this play a regression was activated, which seems to me to be the condition for attaining a psychological symmetry with the German generals. He took a series of photographs of this "game" and apart from their desolate and derelict atmosphere, our attention is again captured by the compulsive repetitive element. Kiefer is not afraid of repeating himself. It is this obsessive repetition, almost to the point of possession, which can be posited as the fuel that fires the psyche into making an image. It could also be a way to activate the instinct of reflection (CW8: 241).

In *Operation Sea Lion I,* 1975 (page 22), with a macabre dramatism and, at the same time, an ironic humor, Kiefer makes an image of the German generals, with the massed troops behind and, in the foreground, the little boats in the bathtub. Above are three empty chairs, which would seem to signify an absent or meaningless Trinity, denoting a very unconscious state. The images in this painting transmit the infinite human capacity for engaging in stupid games when possessed by power, with its consequences of evil and destruction. The generals are intent on their omnipotent game, revealing not only their madness but also their stupidity. Nazism is not only the paradigm of evil, it is the paradigm of stupidity.

This represents a psychological movement: a door is opened into the exploration of the shadow of the stupidity in human nature. We shift the view of

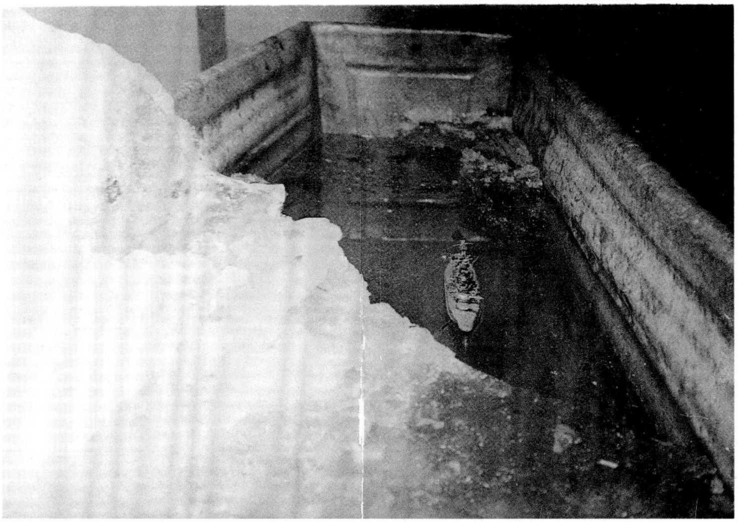

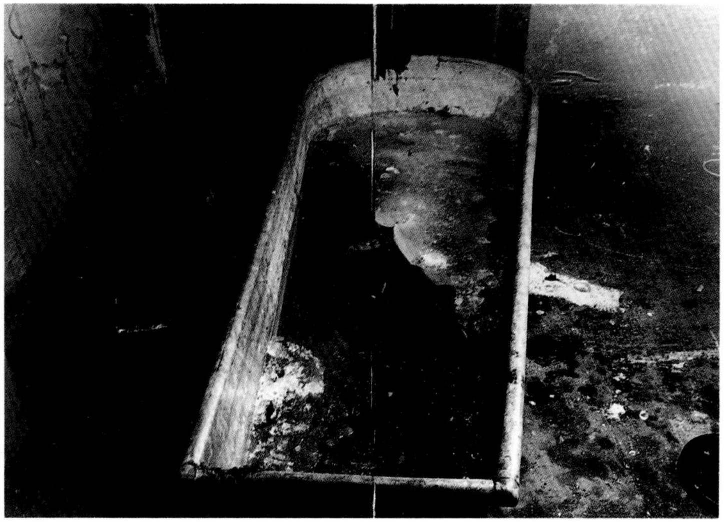

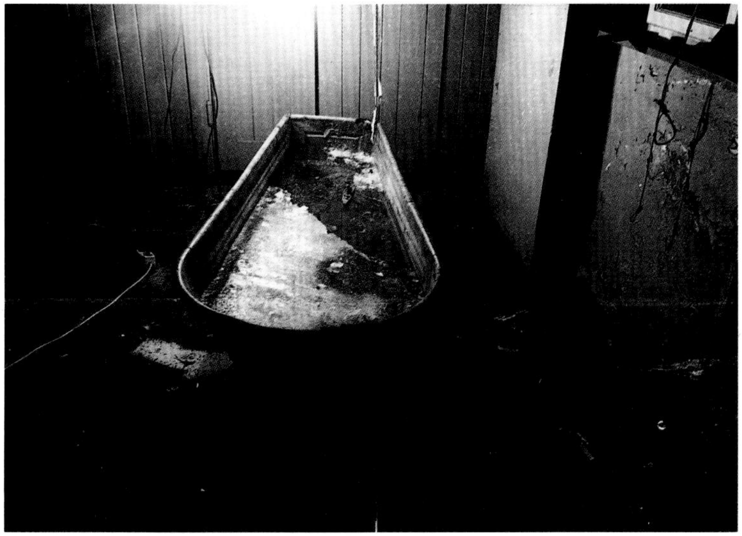

**Operation Sea Lion**
1975

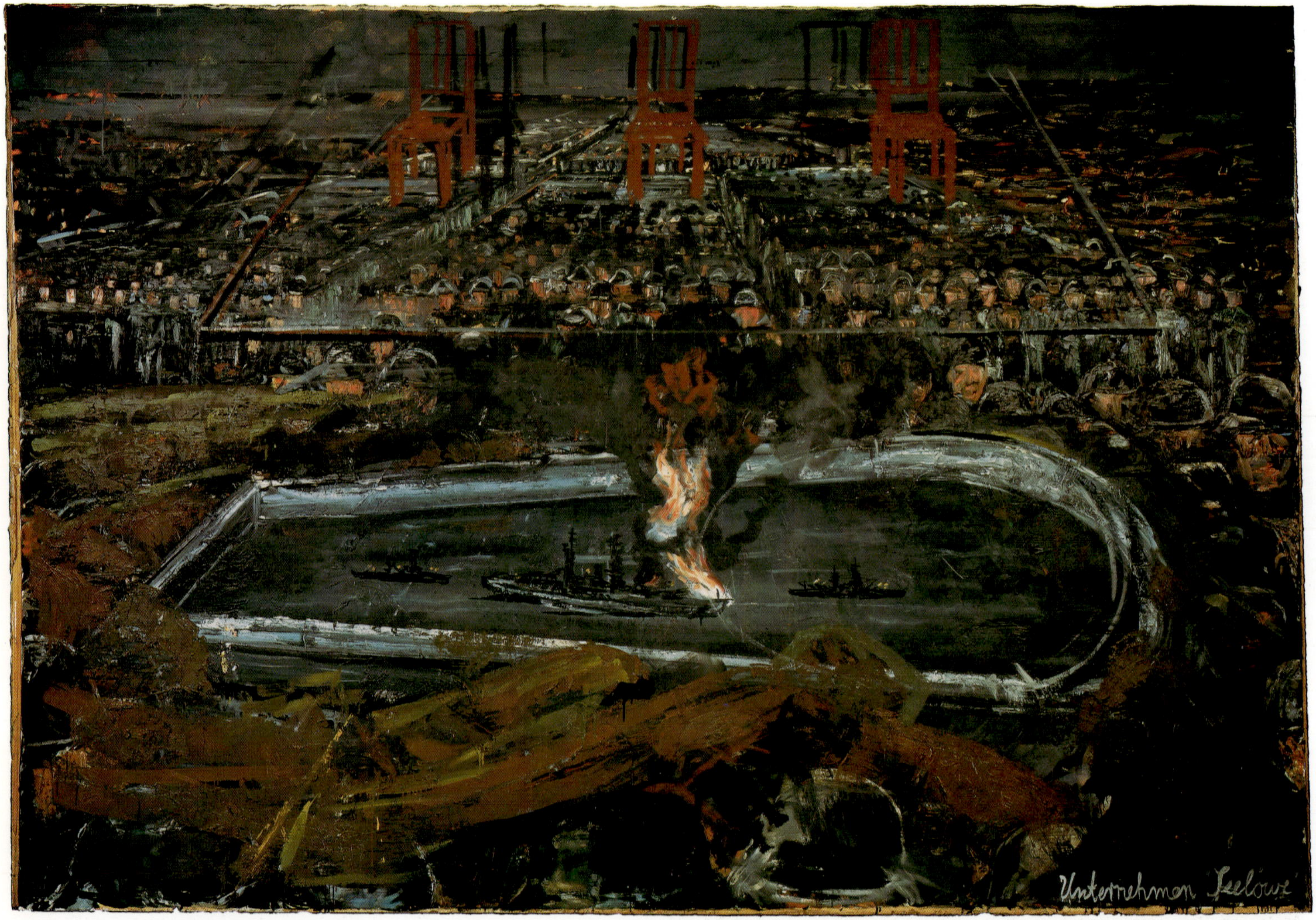


**Operation Sea Lion I,** 1975

evil away from demented Western Manicheanism to a more psychological one, allowing us to perceive stupidity in relation to power.

Kiefer's ability to depict in such a graphic way stupidity as possession by power introduces him as a great psychologist. Modern psychology has failed to discuss sheer stupidity as a relevant part of human nature, as a characteristic human trait. And, here, following Kiefer, I would like to stress that I am reflecting the specific stupidity that is concomitant with power.[3]

In a photograph that appears in his book *To Genet*, Kiefer brings together both the Nazi salute and the bathtub of *Operation Sea Lion I*. Here he is making his Nazi salute standing on the water in a bathtub.

In his essay "After the Catastrophe," Jung wrote:

> the fate of Germany should not mislead Europeans into nursing the illusion that the whole world's wickedness is localized in Germany. They should realize that the German catastrophe was only one crisis in the general European sickness (CW10: 437).

Jung does not let Europe off the hook: he makes a plea for the European to become conscious of his shadow and thus accept his own guilt for the catastrophe. We have to remember that Jung wrote this essay in 1945, in his old age and immediately after the catastrophe, when he brought not only his outrage but also a strong moral stance to his reflections. Kiefer, twenty-four in 1969, reflected

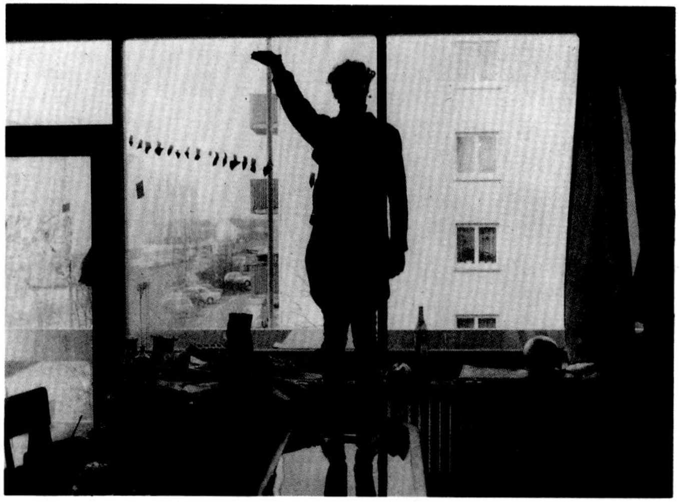

**To Genet**
1969

the catastrophe in another way. He brought all his imagination, irony and sarcasm to his presentation of the Nazi salute standing on the water of a bathtub, an image that displays the most inflated side of the Christian legacy, that madness in which magic, the savior, and the hero meet. We have to appreciate how, through the economy of a body-image, he makes a reflection concerning the failure of our civilization.

Kiefer's paintings, above all the large canvases, with their themes taken from the history of culture, their unique conception of space, and their many sources, have a tremendous emotional impact upon the viewer, even on one who has little connection to this century's art. However, for an approach to Kiefer's intentions and for a fuller comprehension of his work, it is necessary to have some idea of the cultural background of the painting in question. In other words, in Kiefer's art, emotion and intellect are not separate.

A painting such as *Iconoclastic Controversy,* 1980, reawakens and actualizes the historical issue on which the work is based: an extreme intolerance for religious images.[4] During the eighth century, Iconoclasm went to the extremity of killing the Orthodox monks for painting religious images. The movement itself lasted for more than a century (726–843). Arnold Toynbee has studied the outbreak of extreme intolerance in the Iconoclastic Movement, tracing the phenomenon from its first appearance in Byzantine times to our own era. He writes: "The most celebrated school of Iconoclasm is the 'totalitarian' one that is represented by Judaism and, in imitation of Judaism, by Islam" (1946: 519). He surveys not only iconoclasm in religious art, but also the burning of books, which has the same psychological origin. The most famous burning was ordered by the caliph 'Umar:

> [He] is reported to have written, in a reply to an enquiry from a general who had just received the surrender of the city of Alexandria and had asked for instructions as to how he was to dispose of the famous library:
>
> "If these writings of the Greeks agree with the Book of God, they are useless and need not be preserved; if they disagree, they are pernicious and ought to be destroyed" (1946: 518).

Toynbee goes on to say: "In our own day Hitler has done what he can in the way of book-burning" (1946: 518–19). We can also see *Iconoclastic Controversy* as Kiefer's response to the suppression of modern German expressionist art, that which Hitler called "degenerative art."

In *Iconoclastic Controversy,* 1980 (page 25), Kiefer depicts a palette, outlined on a wooden floor, on which there is a battle of little tanks among spurts of white flames. At the same time, the palette, emblem of his creative art, can be viewed as a spider's web, suggesting that art can become either an expression of psychological creativity or become trapped in the web of controversy. Rosenthal (1987: 79) says, "The 1980 depiction [of *Iconoclastic Controversy*] was the culmination of two years work," which I take to mean the period Kiefer studied the implications of the Iconoclastic Controversy. There is no doubt that he has a deep awareness of iconoclasm and is able to perceive it in modern history, in the visual arts, and, because of the palette, in himself. His series of photographs on the Nazi salute was misunderstood in Germany:

> Kiefer's preoccupation with the Iconoclastic Controversy in 1980 coincided with . . . actual events in his own life. His art was the subject of a retrospective exhibition at the German pavilion at the Venice Biennale that year, an event that provoked heated critical attacks from his countrymen. Kiefer was seen as "flaunting his

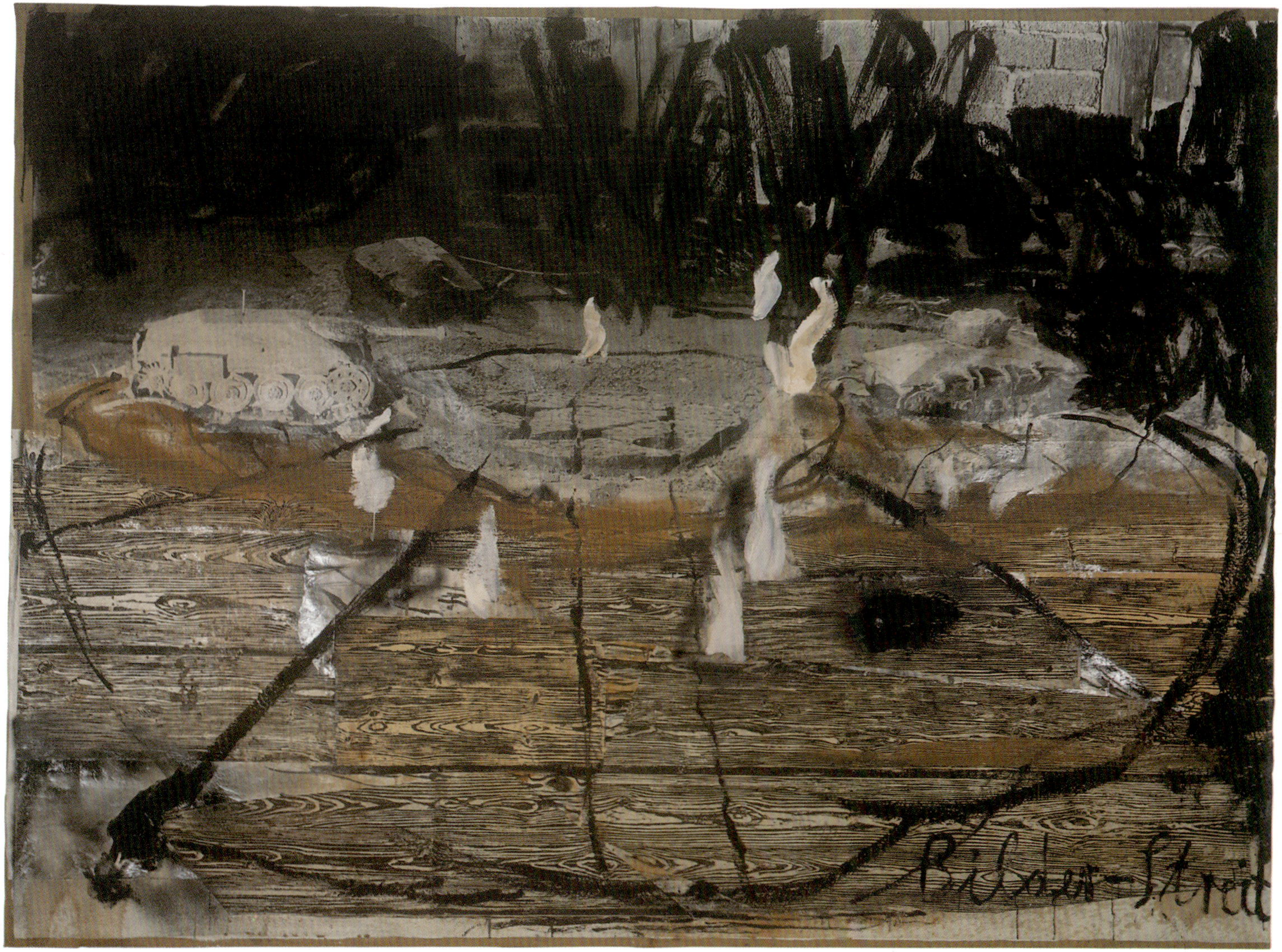


**Iconoclastic Controversy,** 1980

> Germanness" and "flirting with the ghosts of the Fatherland." Kiefer's subject matter . . . uncovered taboos in a German society that preferred current issues and events to those of the past. Remarkably, some even accused him of being a Neo-Nazi . . . . Hence, even in 1980, art continued to be a troublesome thorn in the side of society, much as it had been during the Byzantine period (Rosenthal, 1987: 79).

The accusation of neo-Nazism demonstrates guilt-making in action. Guilt-making is another way iconoclasm functions: it substitutes the image with guilt. These German reactions to Kiefer show that the reflective nature of his work has not been perceived. The German establishment can be said to have an intolerant iconoclastic attitude towards Kiefer's images. But then, they are images that touch deeply the wounds of the German viewer.

In 1980, the same year Kiefer painted the large *Iconoclastic Controversy,* he made a book, *Iconoclastic Controversy II.* There, in a series of photographs (pages 27–29), we see sand and dried grass strewn on his studio floor, where he creates a battle of little tanks in a desert. The palette recurs as a motif; sometimes it is bleeding, as if wounded by the controversy; in the final image it is smashed into scattered fragments. He has written the dramatis personae of the original Byzantine drama on the photographs: Leon III, who took a public stand against icons, Nikephoros I, Michael III, etc. and Irene, the Empress who instigated the restoration of iconophile doctrine. Kiefer has gone to the historical sources of the controversy, which show the demented response given to images under religious pretexts. In so doing he has evidently thought deeply about images and how conflictive they can be in the psyche.

The painting *Iconoclastic Controversy* moves one to consider the psychological dynamism of the image, the effect of which can provoke intolerance or the extreme reaction of iconoclasm. In my essay "Cultural Anxiety," I discuss Western man's anxiety engendered by the conflict between polytheism, with its wealth of images, and monotheism, with its suppression of images (López-Pedraza, 1990). Ten years after writing this essay, I can say that the anxiety to which I referred then has a wider connotation with the insight provided by Kiefer's painting and the possibility he offers to discuss the dementia called iconoclasm. In fact, it is difficult to accept the psychological truth that an image can drive one mad. According to the line of thought we have been following, the destruction generated by iconoclasm can also be associated with an outburst of psychopathic inferiority as the eighth-century Byzantine episode demonstrates. It is only by reflecting on such extreme examples of iconoclasm that we can begin to appreciate the profound effect of an image. This painting is compelling from a psychological perspective because it conveys Kiefer's introjection of the Iconoclastic Controversy, thus turning the historical example into a personal psychological conflict.

I believe that in any inner imaginative process —any image-making—a conflict is present. Our psyche, be it in waking states or in dreams, is constantly involved in controversy; it is perhaps out of this tension between our images and our iconoclasm that the creative process comes.

It is the intellectual and historical background of the painting that makes Kiefer so fascinating for the study of psychology. *Iconoclastic Controversy* touches my interest in psychotherapy, where I consider the image to be of paramount importance. There is a great deal to say about the psychology of intolerance for images, but it would be beyond the scope of this study. Suffice it to say that Kiefer's concern with the issue of iconoclastic controversies challenges us to be aware of the shadow of an intolerance that appears under many guises. For example, modern psychology in general has had little respect for images; in fact, it could be said to have contributed to the historical repression of images by functioning as an iconoclastic system, inasmuch as psychology distorts the natural expression of the psychic image through theories, interpretations, systems, and methods.

It could also be said that such controversies

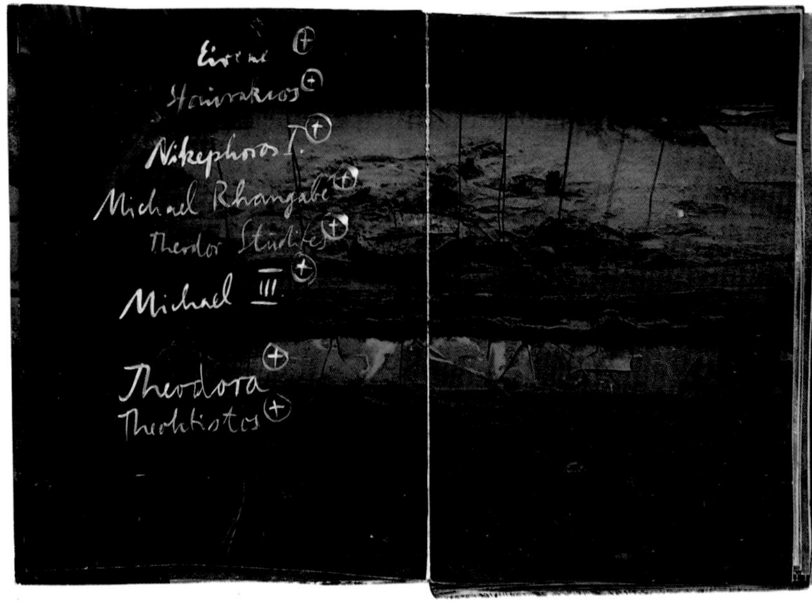


**Iconoclastic Controversy II**
1980

create a constant dynamism in the world of art. In this respect, Kiefer is no doubt bemused by Piet Mondrian, whose work has had a great repercussion in art and architecture. He was an artist who lived a very ascetic monk-like life and put all his energy into abstraction. Kiefer seems to have appreciated how Mondrian takes an image of a tree, for example, and in a series of paintings, bit by bit, reduces it to a few lines.[5] Mondrian's exercise has been seen as spiritual and puritanical, imbued with theosophy and Eastern thought, but we can also see this abstraction as an iconoclastic process, one more step in the systematic Western repression of the image, which is also a repression of the archetypal and instinctive sap of nature. In his painting *Piet Mondrian—Arminius's Battle*, 1976 (page 30),

Iconoclastic Controversy II

1980

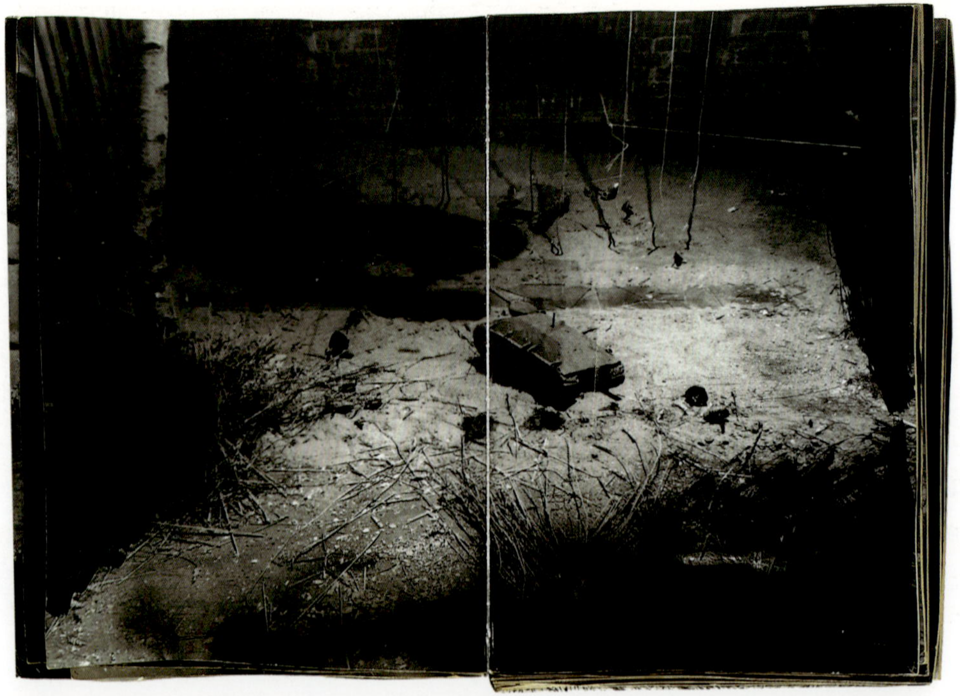

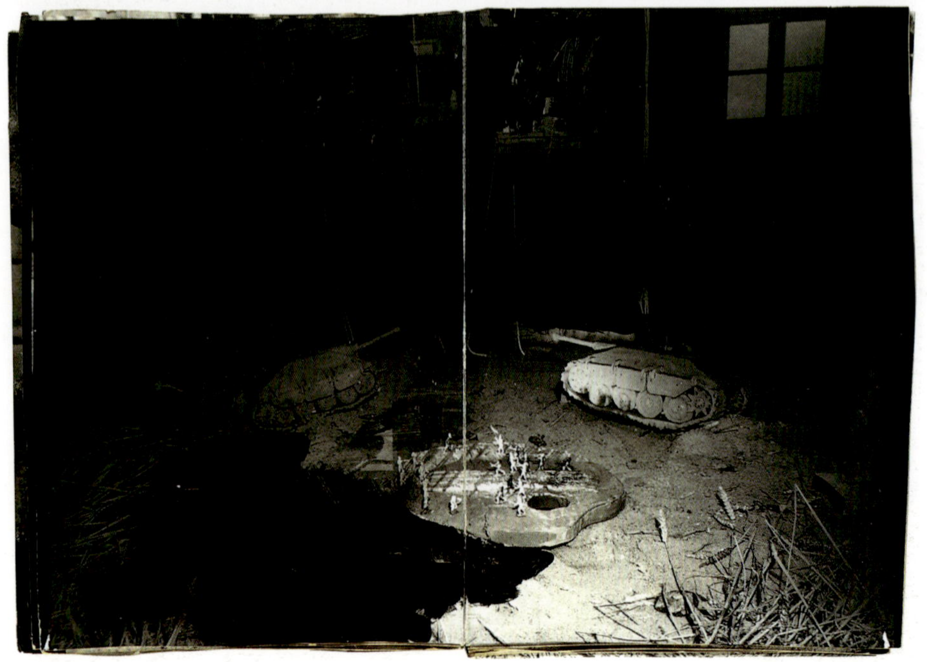

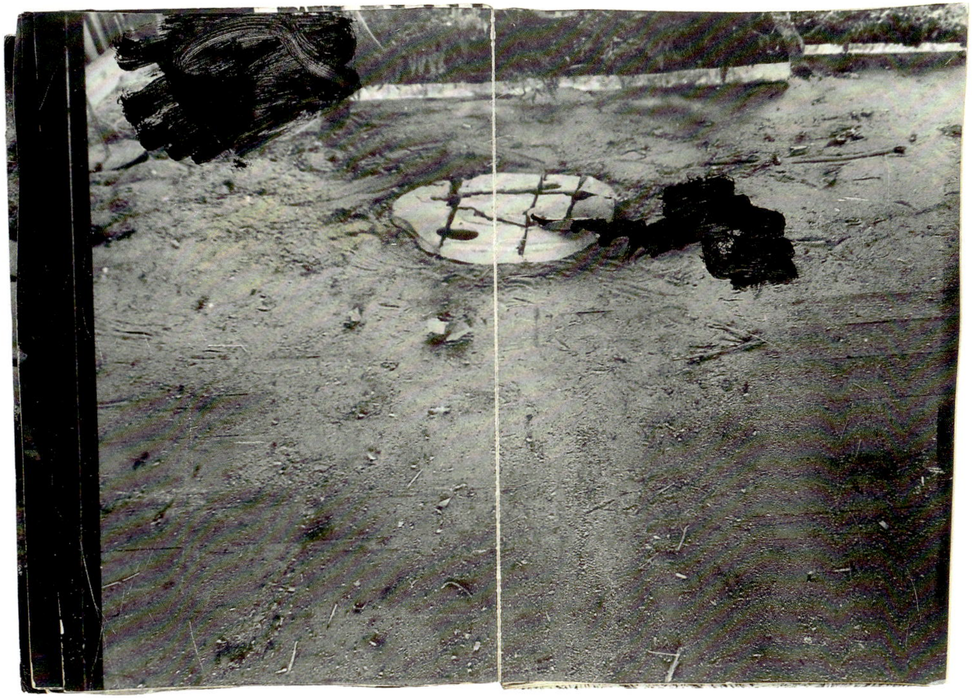

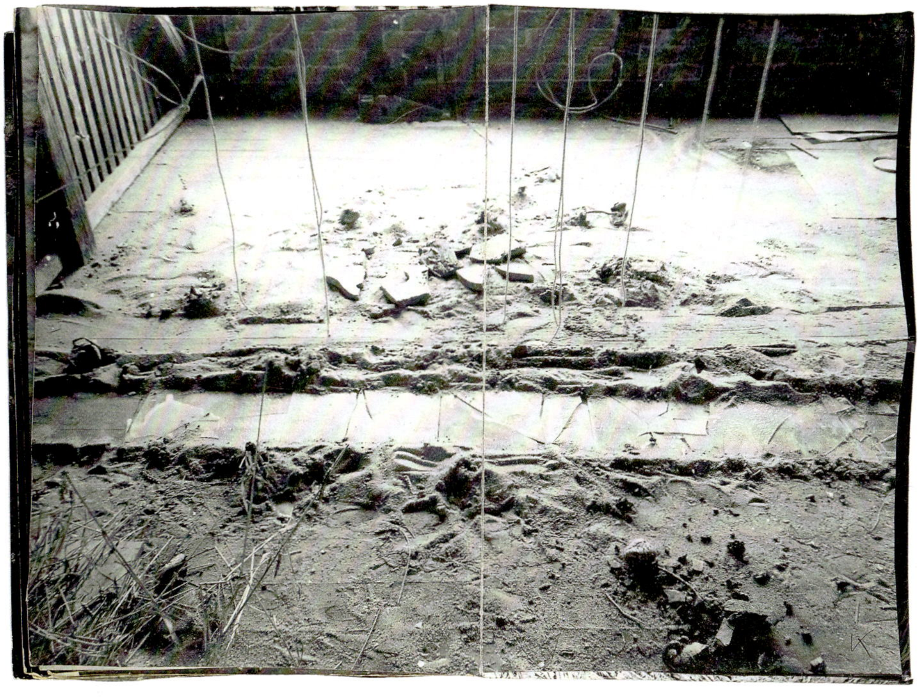

**Iconoclastic Controversy II**
1980

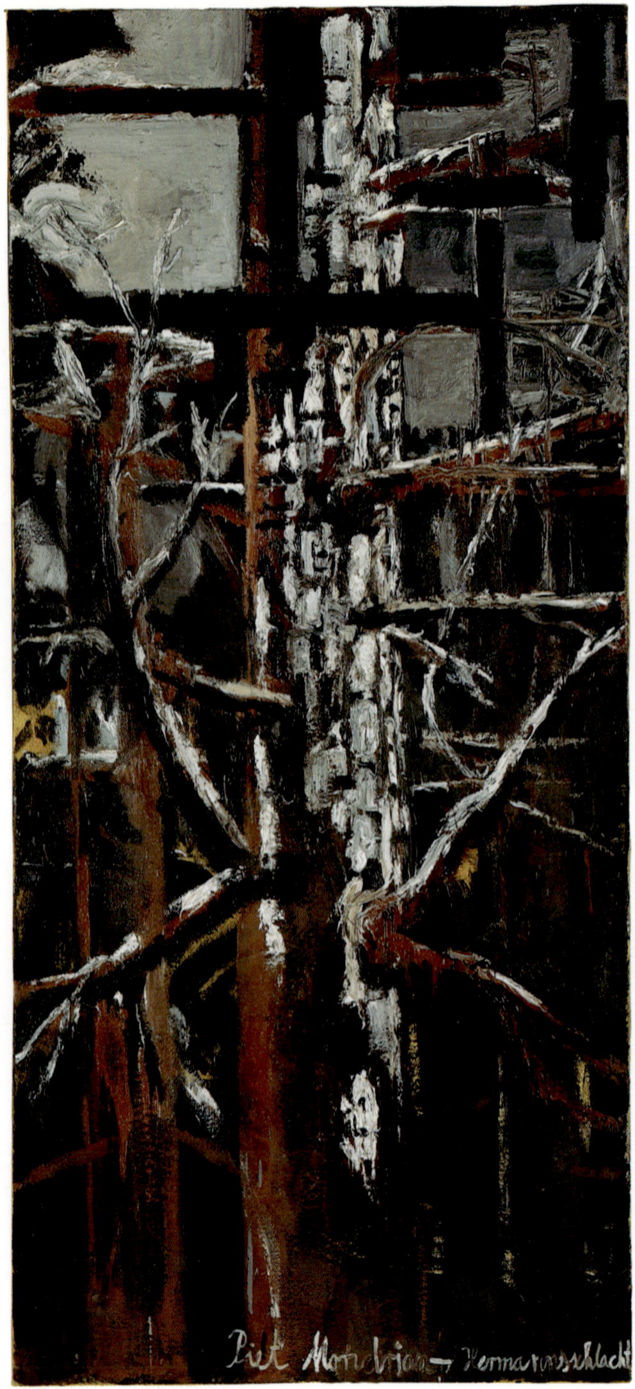


**Piet Mondrian—Arminius's Battle**
1976

Kiefer paints part of a solitary, snow-covered, leafless tree, manifestly connecting Mondrian to the strange spiky trees, reminiscent of the trees in the Teutoberg Forest, where the ancient German's battle took place, motifs that appear in so many of Kiefer's paintings of this period. Here we can see a reversal of Mondrian's abstraction of the tree. It seems Kiefer is putting Mondrian back into this sort of primordial wintry forest at the roots of the German nature, at the dawn of German history.

In the summer of 1974, Kiefer traveled overland to North Cape, the northernmost part of Norway. It seems to have been both an instinctive and intuitive search for the roots and the very locale of the Norse legends, the sources of German mythology. As aides-mémoire along the way, he recorded the topography, icebergs, and sunsets with a Polaroid camera and also collected postcards. Kiefer evidently brooded on and played with all these collected images before embarking on the impressive watercolors of the book *Erotik im Fernen Osten oder: Transition from cool to warm.* This book is presented in *A Book by Anselm Kiefer,* 1988, the cover of which is a replica of the original. In the introduction, Theodore E. Stebbins and Susan Cragg Ricci explain the perishable quality of Kiefer's book:

> The watercolors here are simple and direct; they contain no written signs or text, and no second level of imagery. Yet Kiefer accomplishes his aim—offering us and then withdrawing the beautiful object—in other ways. For example, the paper he used is pulpy and low-quality, providing the book with a sense of its own mortality. The binding is poor, and the paper thin and fragile, so that each person who handles it hastens its end, just as when one touches a delicate flower. Moreover, the artist has painted the watercolors on the front and back of many pages, so it is impossible to take the book apart in order to display it. In addition, Kiefer has given the book multiple levels of meaning that slowly become apparent through his sequential treatment of the watercolors: to see just one page out of context is to drain the meaning of it (1988: 20).

Later, as we shall see, Kiefer's monumental *Zweistromland,* a library made of lead, transmits the feeling of durability, to the extent of being able to survive even a nuclear war. Such opposites, taken together, allow us to speculate as to what they might mean in terms of Kiefer's psychology.

I shall discuss the first part of the book, recording his trip to Norway, because it is profoundly relevant to the subjects in Kiefer's work that I address in this study. Kiefer's trip to Norway could be seen as a *peregrinatio,* or pilgrimage, a search for his mythological roots, and also as a quickening of psychic transformations and creative processes. It even gives us the possibility to see this trip to the north within the imagination of the alchemists, who affiliated the four elements to the four continents: to Africa was attributed the element of fire; to Asia, air; to America, water; and to Europe, earth. Lastly, they projected upon the fifth continent, Australia, the quintessence. However, they brought an even more audacious imagination to bear on their fascination with the magnetic pull of the North Pole and they projected onto the frigid polar regions some deep unconscious contents. In *Aion*, Jung cites the following alchemical text from the "Introitus apertus" of the writer known as Philalethes:

> In the Pole is found the heart of Mercurius, "which is the true fire wherein its Lord has his rest. He who journeys through this great and wide sea may touch at both Indies, may guide his course by the sight of the North Star, which our Magnet will cause to appear unto you." This is an allusion to the mystic journey, the "peregrinatio" (CW9ii: 206).

Jung stresses the significance of the *peregrinatio* to the North Pole for the alchemist:

> the infernal fire is nothing other than the *Deus absconditus* (hidden god) who dwells at the North Pole and reveals himself through magnetism. His other synonym is Mercurius, whose heart is to be found at the Pole, and who guides men on their perilous voyage over the sea of the world. The idea that the whole machinery of the world is driven by the infernal fire at the North Pole, that this is hell, and that hell is a system of upper powers reflected in the lower—this is a shattering thought (CW9ii: 209).

The North Pole was also thought of as the abode of Lucifer, the cold regions of evil, and came to symbolize a special madness. The series of watercolors with which Kiefer recorded his trip to the northernmost tip of Norway suggests this kind of alchemical imagination.[6]

The alchemists' imagination about the northernmost region of the Pole appears in modern dreams. A psychiatrist in mid-life who was working with severely mentally ill patients told me the following dream: "I was working in the laboratory of the clinic, studying through a microscope a green substance from the North Pole that contained a specific madness." It was indeed this dream that fed my imagination in relation to Kiefer's probable state of mind, the inner turmoil he provoked in himself by this journey north to seek out and activate the German mythological roots in his own soul. The dream can be seen as an analogy to Kiefer's trip to North Cape, and we can imagine him, upon his return, processing in his inner laboratory the madness coming out of the North Pole. It is noteworthy that Kiefer carried out such a northward journey, with its implications of the magnetic pull of the North Pole and the extreme cold, with the alchemical fire at its heart.

That Kiefer achieved his objective with this *peregrinatio* to the north, this activation of

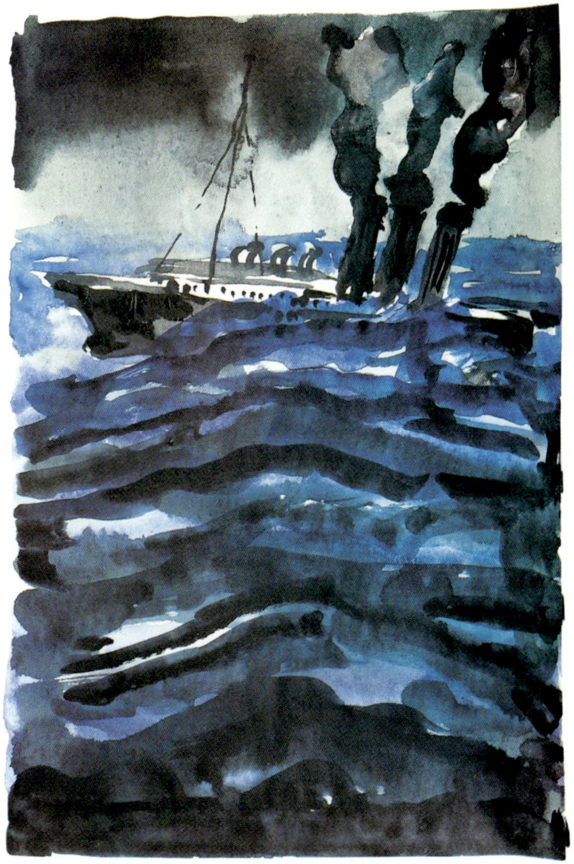

**Erotik im Fernen Osten**
1975

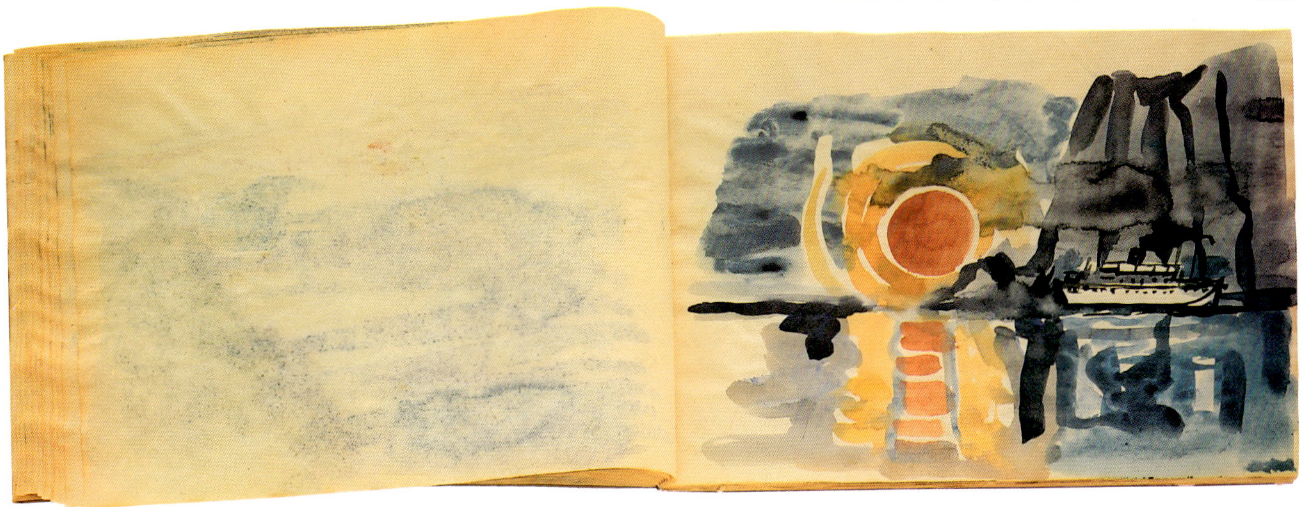

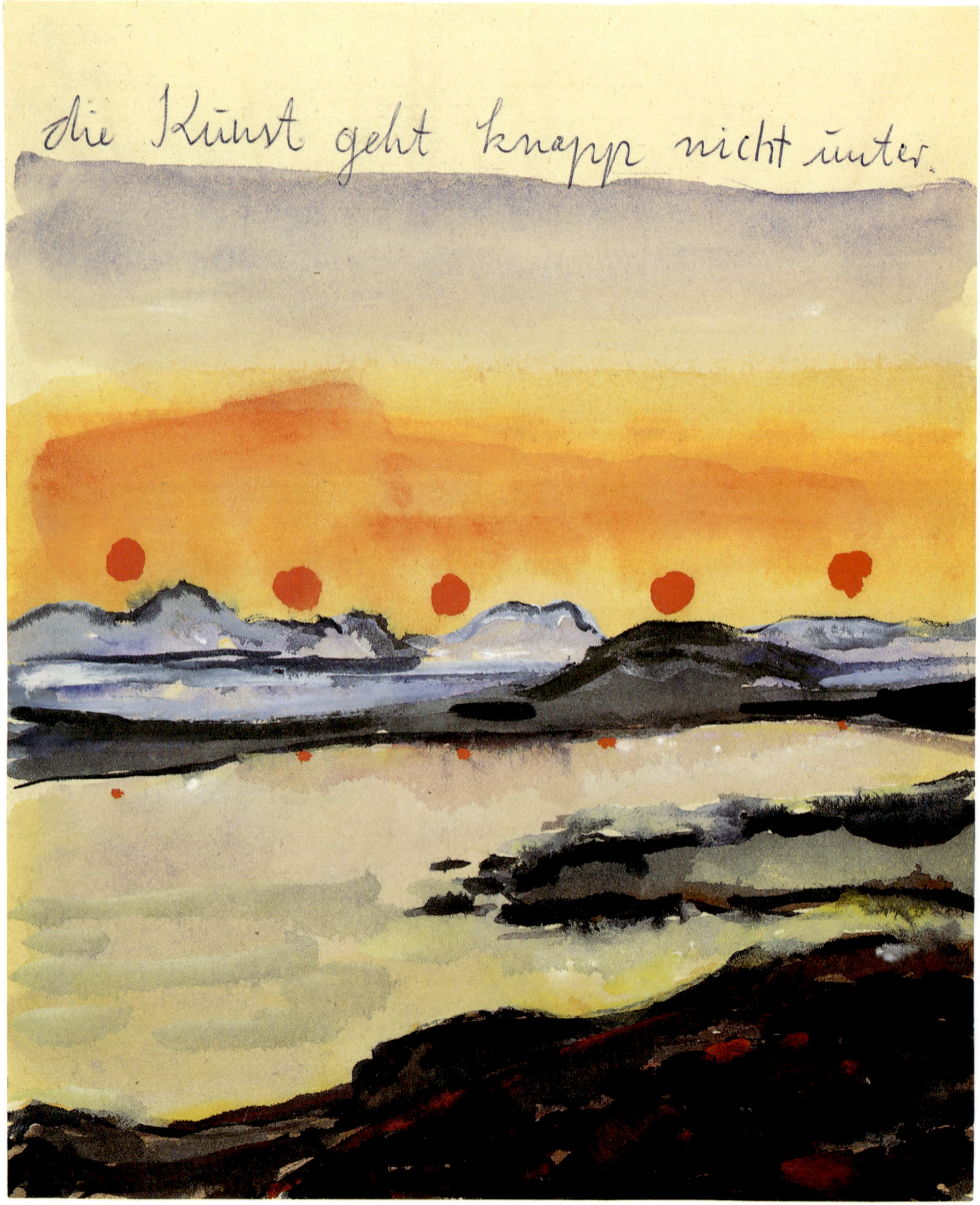


**North Cape**
1975

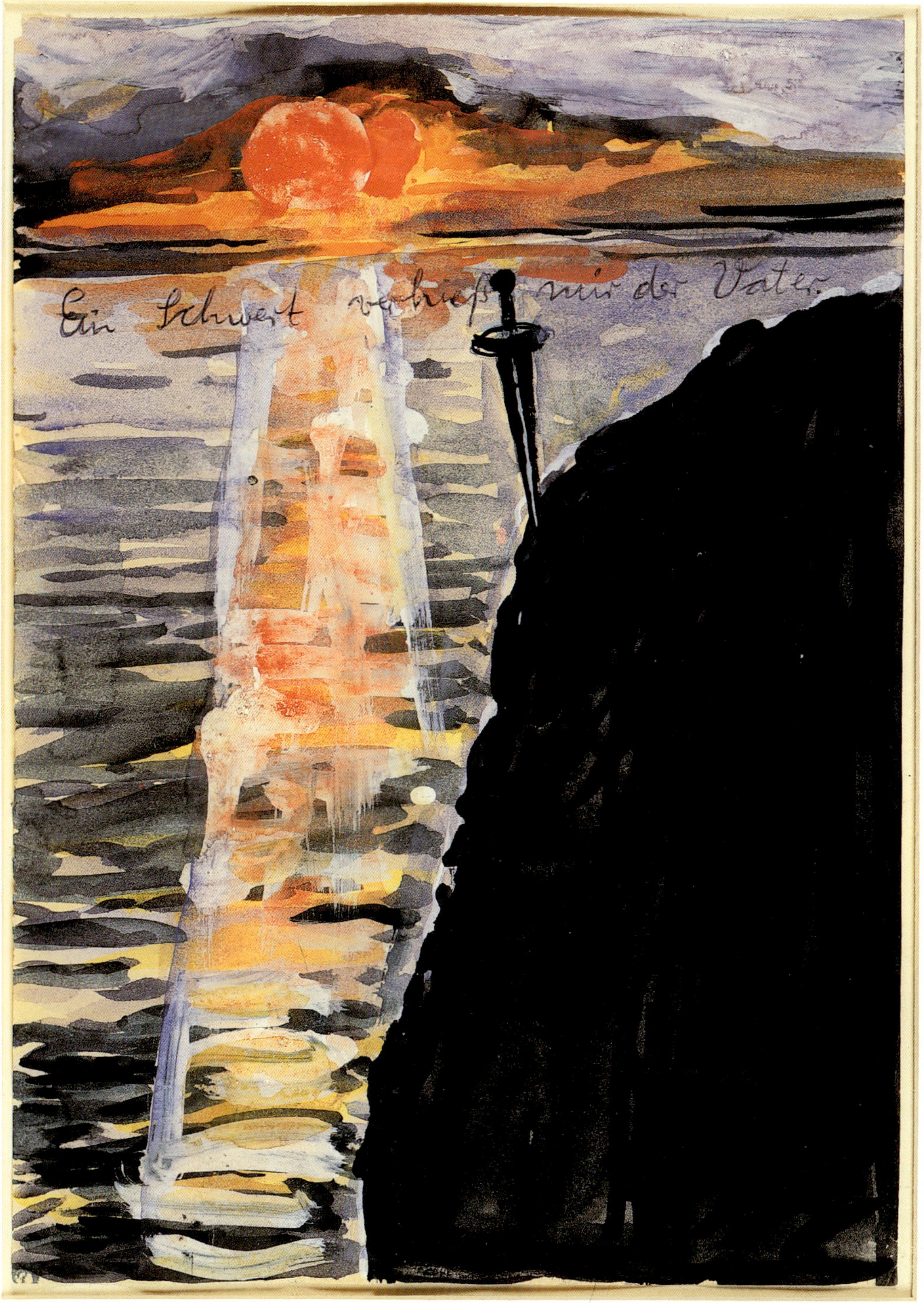


**My Father Promised Me a Sword,** 1974

unconscious psychic contents, is attested to in a series of paintings he produced in the years after the trip, with themes from German mythology and history. As a record of the trip itself, he did a series of beautiful and fascinating watercolors that comprise the first part of the book *Erotik im Fernen Osten* (page 33). We see a ship, symbolizing Kiefer's psychological vehicle (or container), plowing through the frigid seas. Then the scene is flooded with the red light of the polar sun and the spell is broken, awakening a primordial awareness. A later watercolor, *North Cape,* 1975 (page 34), with the words "die Künst geht knapp nicht unter" (art doesn't just disappear) written across the sky, seems to be Kiefer's last view of the northern regions. We see a rather hallucinatory landscape: five red polar suns are setting, or rising, from behind low icy hills, and they send their rays over the desolate Luciferian region of the alchemists' imagination.

*My Father Promised Me a Sword,* 1974 (page 35), is evidence that Kiefer found what he had pursued on this trip north. Here we see the scenery of North Cape depicted as if it were the dawn of creation; to the right a sword sticks out of a black mass of rock. We know this is Wotan's sword because, a year before in 1973, Kiefer had already produced an oil painting *Nothung,* 1973 (page 37), in which the conceptualized subtitle: "My father promised me a sword" points to an intuition.

In Wagner's version of the myth, Wotan promised his son, Siegmund, a sword that would be invincible in battle. Siegmund christened this sword Nothung. Later Wotan shattered the sword with his spear and Siegmund died. Siegfried, Siegmund's son, inherited the fragments of the sword which, as a fearless hero, only he was able to reforge. The first thing he did with the recast sword was to split the anvil in two.

Robert Donnington states that Wotan should be understood as the father-image in German mythology (1963: 71–72), meaning that the inheritance of the sword transfers Wotan's forces. In Kiefer's painting, the sword is bloody, and so this would seem to point to the blood inheritance of the German people. The wooden room, a place Kiefer has used in many of his paintings, was inspired by his atelier at that time, an abandoned school in his hometown of Buchen. His rendering of this room transmits a very powerful emotion and his placement of the sword in his own atelier could well have to do with the introverted side of his personality, an introversion that can withstand a limited, claustrophobic space and accommodate the internalization of the image of the myth with which his psyche is occupied. In the watercolor *My Father Promised Me a Sword,* painted after his trip, his earlier intuition seems to have been confirmed: he places that same sword at its mythological and psychological source in the frigid regions of the

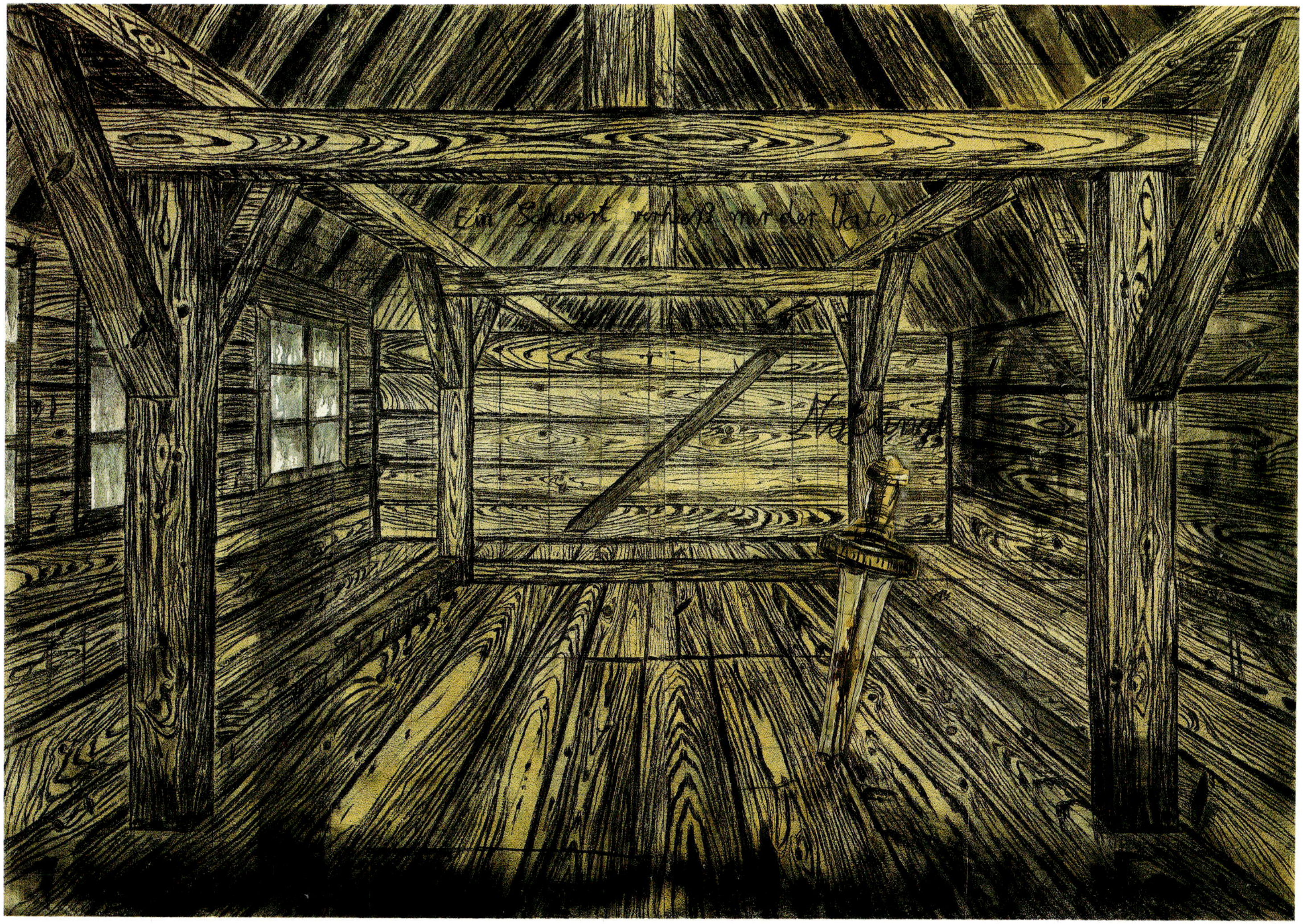


**Nothung,** 1973

north. This depiction of Wotan's sword is an artistic expression of a reflection similar to that of Jung in his essay on Wotan. Here is a meeting of psychiatry and art, each having the purpose of getting in touch with the "particular biology" of the German Wotanic nature.

The enormous painting *Parsifal II,* 1973 (page 39), is Kiefer's depiction of a great European myth, one that contains a strong theme of redemption. I would like to quote the vivid and emotional reaction to this powerful work that an old friend and colleague wrote to me after seeing this painting in the Zürich Kunsthaus:

> Then I found this socking great Kiefer! Its size alone is moving. Let me tell you what I saw. What it means I have no idea!: An enormous claustrophobic wooden room with no windows; empty, threatening and unpleasantly uncanny. Two monstrous constructions of wooden beams in the room doing nothing and reminiscent of gallows. A bucket of blood in the middle, such as you might see at a butcher's. Amfortas is down below in spirit and unredeemed. Parsifal is up in the air in spirit. The myth doesn't seem to work, and the myth not working is a claustrophobic building with pompous constructions —empty.

My friend's commentary on Kiefer's *Parsifal* is a beautiful example of the reading of an image. His statement that the painting depicts a myth that does not work is striking; it suggests that the myth once functioned but now does not, making us wonder about Kiefer's intention in depicting the myth through an image of horror. Furthermore it challenges our thoughts about myth itself.

The myth of Parsifal is composed of a mixture of fairy tale motifs, Celtic folklore, and, above all, the legend of the Holy Grail. The blood flowing from the wound in the side of the crucified Jesus, pierced by the spear of the Roman soldier Longinus, was caught in this vessel held up by Joseph of Arimathea. The legend also told that it was this cup from which Jesus and his disciples drank at the Last Supper. From the eighth century through the Middle Ages, the powerful emotion of this legend made it a literary motif that fed the medieval imagination. It was the foundation of the literature of chivalry, which ranged from the Arthurian legends to *Don Quixote.* The two greatest writers of the Parsifal (Perceval, Parzifal) myth were Chretién de Troyes (1135–1183) and Wolfram von Eschenbach (1170–1220). The many versions of the Parsifal myth and the ample literature on chivalry were crucial for the flowering of the European languages—Scandinavian, English, French, German, Spanish, and Portuguese. Parsifal became an important model for ethical and civilized behavior for the autochthonous European, and so aided one's assimilation of Christianity. Emma Jung spent thirty years on a psychological interpretation of the wealth of symbolism contained in the legend of the Holy Grail, seeing in

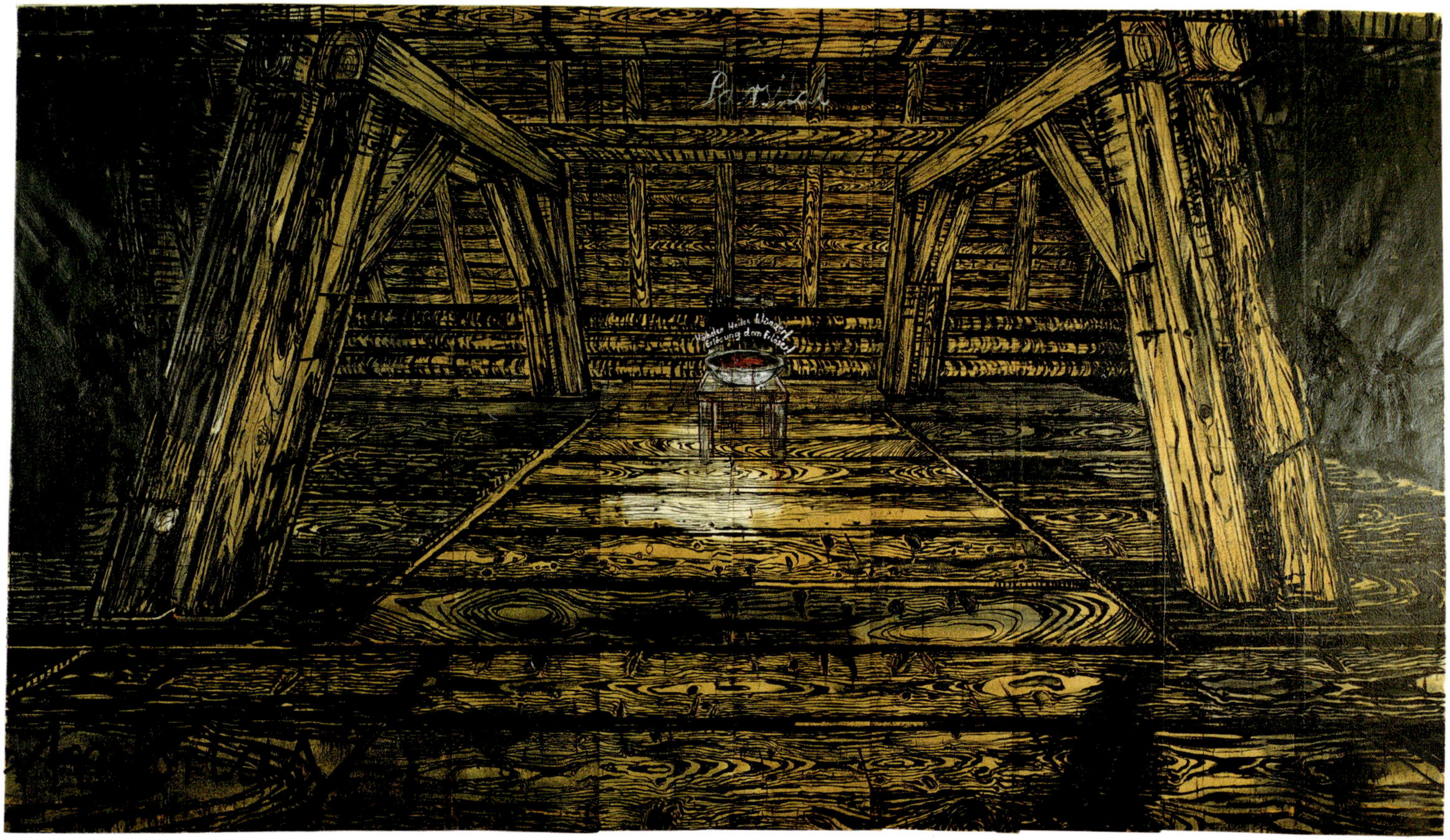

**Parsifal II,** 1973

Parsifal a personification of the inner life, feeling values, and individuation. So now we can begin to understand the reaction of my friend, a well-educated European man, who was acquainted with the motif of a myth that had worked throughout many centuries of European culture.

It is in this painting that Kiefer begins to express openly the psychology of "after the catastrophe." His reflection of the myth is direct and dramatic: the wooden claustrophobic room; the bucket of blood, a modern substitute for the Holy Grail; and the names of the myth's two main protagonists, Amfortas, the wounded King, and Parsifal, the foolish pure hero. It is an image of horror, transmitting a unique emotion. Kiefer's rendering of *Parsifal* confronts us with a myth that does not function. On the other hand, we can say Kiefer's image of horror does function. In *Hermes and His Children*, I addressed the image of horror as a psychic mover, quoting Frances Yates in relation to the value that medieval man gave to such images:

> And now the *imagines agentes* make their appearance, quoted in full from Tullius. Remarkably beautiful or hideous, dressed in crowns and purple garments, deformed or disfigured with blood or mud, smeared with red paint, comic or ridiculous, they stroll mysteriously, like players, out of antiquity into the scholastic treatise on memory as part of Prudence. The solution emphasizes that the reason for the choice of such images is that they "move strongly" and so adhere to the soul (1989: 159).

Kiefer reveals himself as a great artist in his treatment of an image of horror: his indirection makes him comparable to the great tragedians who knew how to present images of horror and transmit emotion and reflection.

**W**e saw how, with *Parsifal II,* Kiefer boldly tackled a European myth. Now let us see how he approaches a very German myth, the Nibelungen, one that is powerful in the German collective unconscious. Before going further, a bare outline of the myth is necessary and I have not found a better resumé than the one made by Stebbins and Ricci:

> In the Wagnerian version the gold lying deep in the Rhine River, guarded by the Rhine maidens, represents the wealth and power that both men and gods seek; even Wotan, king of the gods, lusts for Alberich's ring, made from the gold, though it is cursed and brings destruction to those who wear it. The Valkyrie Brunhilde has been cast into a deep sleep, where she is protected by a circle of fire against all but the very bravest of men. Siegfried, the hero, slays the dragon who guards the ring, and takes it. A child of nature who has never seen a woman, he understands the wild bird's song, which leads him to Brunhilde's rock. After defeating Wotan in battle, he pierces the flames and awakens Brunhilde. Leaving behind his love, he goes to

> pursue his destiny. He comes to the castle of Gunther, where Hagen (the king's half-brother) is plotting to take the ring. The unsuspecting Siegfried is given a magic potion that makes him forget Brunhilde; he then falls in love with Gunther's sister, Gutrune. Still drugged, he agrees to go to Brunhilde disguised as Gunther to take her as Gunther's bride. After he goes through the fire again and claims her for Gunther, he makes plans to marry Gutrune. Brunhilde, realizing she has been tricked, is enraged and plans revenge on Siegfried. The Rhine maidens urge Siegfried to give back the ring, warning of its dangers, but he refuses. Hagen—urged on by Brunhilde—stabs Siegfried, who in his dying moments regains his memory and proclaims his love for Brunhilde. Brunhilde then realizes that Siegfried is innocent; taking the ring to give back to the Rhine maidens, she rides her horse, Grane, into Siegfried's burning funeral pyre, proclaiming their love. Flames then engulf Valhalla, palace of the gods, and the gods are thus destroyed; at the end, the Rhine rises and floods the scene (1988: 24–25).

Wagner brings tragic features to his operatic version of the Nibelungen, which he based on the poems of the Edda and on the anonymous medieval epic poem *Nibelungenlied.* His heroes are moved by unconscious forces that make their tragic destiny. Of course, this is basically the conception of Greek tragedy, but the mise-en-scène of Greek tragedy aims at creating emotion in the audience (Stanford, 1983) that brings about a tragic reflection of life (depth psychology). But in Wagner's *Nibelung*, the emotional effect on the audience is quite different: the mythological contents and the music of the opera engender identification with the myth. Reflection does not seem to happen.

It is not difficult to appreciate that the mythological plot of the four operas, comprising Wagner's *The Ring of the Nibelung* and culminating in the story of Siegfried and Brunhilde, consists of one disaster after another, brought about by ambition for gold and power. What is most evident is the myth's fatal outcome and it makes us think again about myth.

As Stebbins and Ricci have observed, the Nibelung myth is an important part of Kiefer's reflections concerning German mythology and history (1988: 24). It was Wagner's portrayal of Siegfried that became Hitler's model for the hero and that was constellated in the German collective at the time of National Socialism, personifying a complex.[7] There was an infatuation, almost an idolatry, with Siegfried. Furthermore, as Kiefer's work implies, Siegfried has now become a personification of the fissure in modern man's psyche: the modern man who has no spiritual or psychological forms for containing eruptions of psychopathic inferiority or, to put it another way, the man who is easily caught by the collective forces of psychopathic inferiority.

Stebbins and Ricci offer some reflections on Kiefer's work from the viewpoint of Jungian psy-

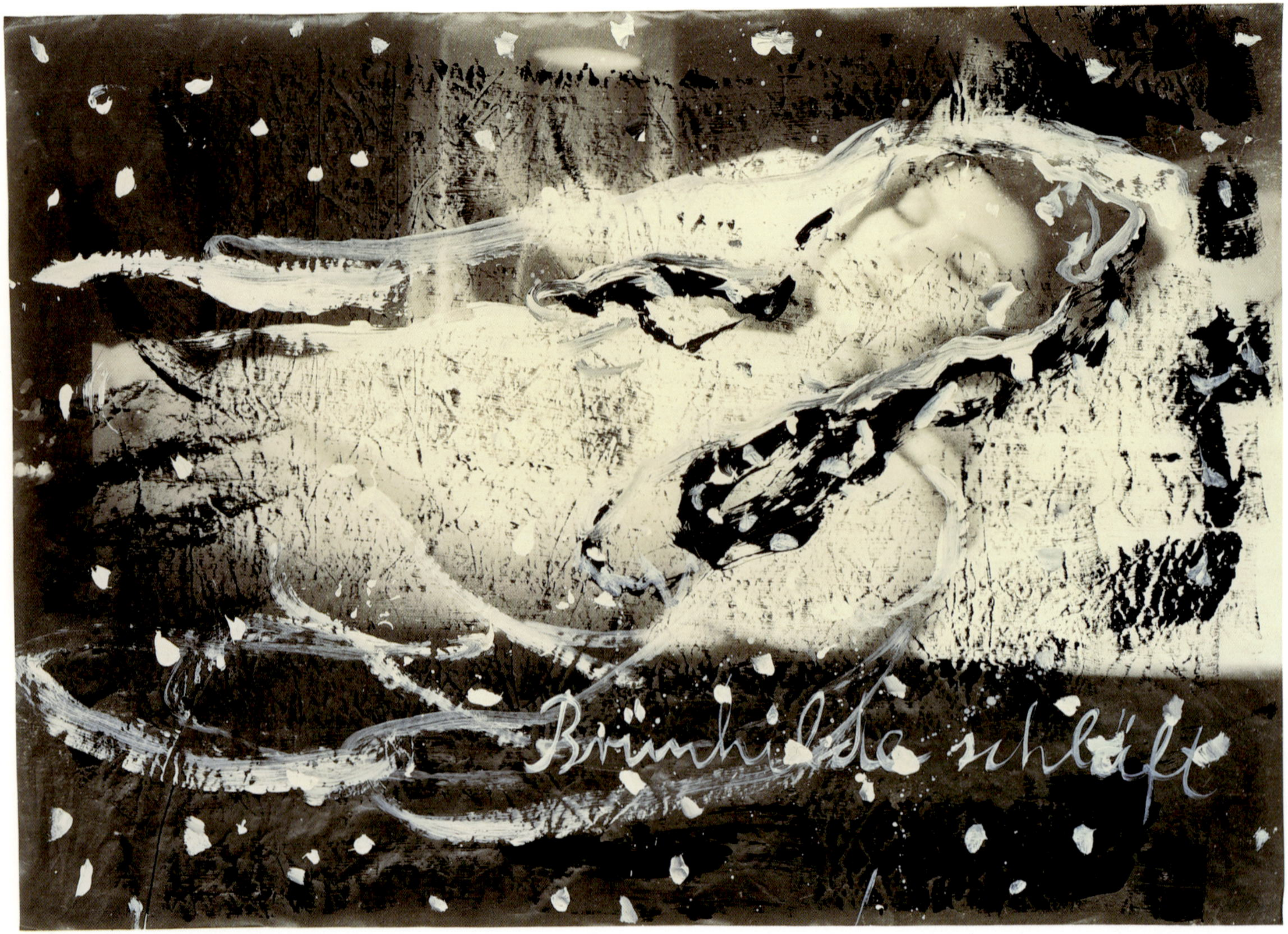


 **Brunhilde Sleeps,** 1980

chology, and Robert Donnington in 1963 interpreted Wagner's version of the myth from a Jungian perspective. Donnington sees Siegfried as a hero, basing his interpretation on Jung's *Symbols of Transformation*, published in 1912, at a time when Jung's interest was to explore the myth of the solar hero. My own approach to the myth is backed by Jung's essays published after World War II, that is to say, "after the catastrophe," thirty-three years later, a time of new insight into the inferior psychopathy of the hero. Between 1912 and 1945 history offered a final lesson on the hero myth, a change that Jung registered in his *Essays on Contemporary Events.*

Kiefer has devoted various works to the myth of Siegfried and Brunhilde. In *Brunhilde Sleeps,* 1980 (page 42), he goes to the myth directly and depicts the sleeping Brunhilde, her first appearance in the myth. But it is in *Siegfried Forgets Brunhilde,* 1975 (page 44), where Kiefer hits on the part of the myth that is most important for modern psychology. Here, Kiefer expresses "forgetting" as a bleak, wintry landscape, with the words "Siegfried vergißt Brunhilde" written along one of the snowy furrows, words echoing in the immensity of a desolate horizon.

In line with Jungian thought and following Donnington, Brunhilde is Siegfried's anima and would be seen as the inner imago of the feminine. In the myth, she is in exclusive opposition to the outer ambition for gold and power. So to forget Brunhilde is to forget the inner life. The archetype of the anima, an inner figure, is often projected upon an actual woman, but is not to be confused with her. In reality, throughout history, women also have been possessed by the ambition for gold and power, thus forgetting their own feminine soul, their own anima. It is not difficult to connect such a state of forgetfulness, in both men and women, to psychopathic inferiority, to the "soulless beings" without an inner life referred to earlier. And, of course, to forget the anima is not an exclusively German problem. However, the strong collective German identification with the Siegfried myth, as was so evident at the time of National Socialism, magnifies the issue in German culture.

Fortunately Kiefer tackles the "forgetting of the anima" as the central motif of a painting, a task no other painter has undertaken, as far as I know. In forgetting Brunhilde, Siegfried reveals his lack of an inner life. In his rejection of the Rhine maidens' warning, we see him in the grip of a demonic possession that cuts him off from any instinctive reflection.

One can, through Jung's conception of the Wotanic force as a peculiar biology, reflect on the difference between biological drive and instinct. Usually, biological drives are seen as pure instinct. Siegfried inherited the Wotanic sword and thus that peculiar biology, leading one to consider a different level of nature than that of

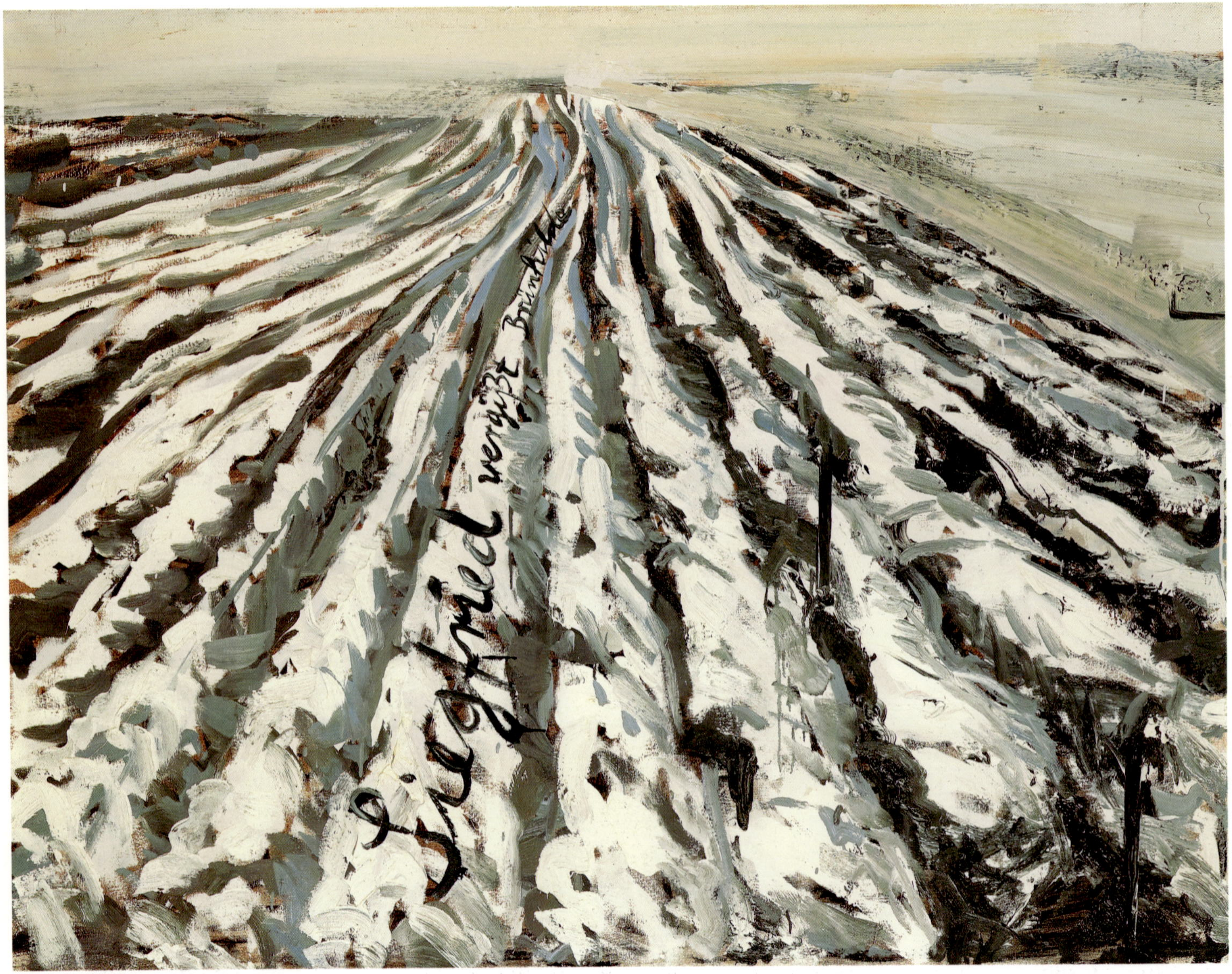


**Siegfried Forgets Brunhilde,** 1975

the instincts. The characters and the plot of the Nibelungen are so full of destruction, and touch the German psyche so deeply, that one imagines a biology that functions independently of the instincts. Siegfried is the hero par excellence in German mythology, and one can only make sense of such an identification with a hero of such a destructive fate by connecting it to the inheritance of that peculiar Wotanic biology.

Stebbins and Ricci draw our attention to the fact that the title of *Siegfried Forgets Brunhilde* is in the present tense; it seems to be important for Kiefer that this mythological theme is expressed in the present. His scenography of the myth is very different from that of Wagner, whose opera, romantic in form and unconscious in content, depicts a mythological time. Kiefer sees the myth in terms of the common man, in the here and now of "after the catastrophe." He reflects these two figures as constant factors in the German psyche, as "Everyman and Everywoman" (Stebbins and Ricci 1988: 27). Thus his vision of the myth brings it closer to the way modern psychotherapy uses myth.

In *Brunhilde and Her Fate,* 1977, Kiefer portrays Brunhilde as a sexy modern woman. He uses pop art, which depicts Brunhilde colloquially and makes her accessible. It could be said that Kiefer sees the theme of Siegfried and Brunhilde as the love affair of a modern young couple; at

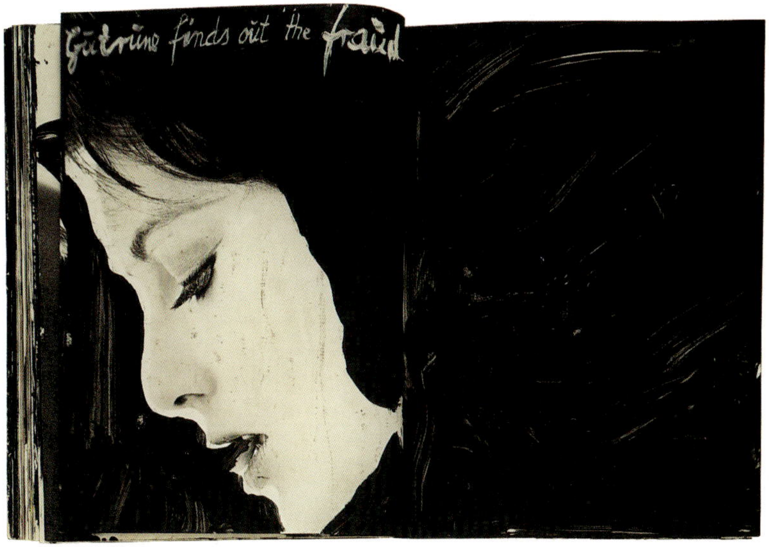


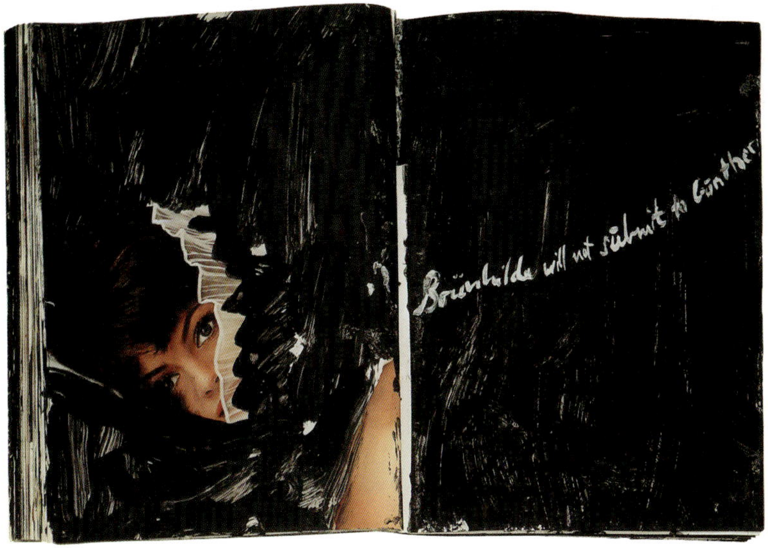


**Brunhilde and Her Fate**
1977

the core of his vision is a psychology based on the living reality of a man and a woman. A commonplace of today is a young man, Siegfried, a hero possessed by ambition and the lure of gold and power—a yuppie?—who is invariably married to a beautiful young woman, with a wealthy father, Brunhilde. The couple falls into drugs, alcohol, spouse-swapping, and all the rest. Their life is all outside, mimetic and robot-like, idealizing celebrity. They have no inner life at all and the anima is totally forgotten. Needless to say, there is no connection to the instincts and their life goes into disaster: illness, jail, death, or even worse, a repetitive life without satisfaction or meaning.

Kiefer's approach to the theme of Siegfried and Brunhilde deflates the whole paraphernalia of an idealized romantic conception of the myth, leading one to speculate as to whether this might not have something of a healing effect on the Germans. Kiefer neither falls into the postwar German psychology of trying to repress its mythology, nor does he succumb to the illusion of an easy redemption of the German historical madness.

During the 1970s and early 1980s Kiefer's work combined German mythological and historical themes. It is his interest in working with both nature and history that makes him such an exceptional artist: he is able to hold together these two opposites and often blends them into one painting such as in *Varus,* 1976 (page 48). The painting depicts the first-century victory of the Germanic hoards under the leadership of Arminius (Hermann) over the Roman legions, commanded by Quintilius Varus, in the Teutoberg Forest.[8] This victory can be seen as marking the beginning of German history, sealing the German destiny. The lands beyond the Rhine were peopled by indigenous tribes who, because of their victory over the Romans, were not included in the European admixture and so remained a "pure" race. This historical fact makes the Germans unique among the major European nations, whose people were basically an ethnic mixture of native, Celt, Germanic, Nordic and Roman invaders, a racial mix that helped to tame the Wotanic element in these nations.

> In *Varus,* Kiefer represents the action-filled narrative in linguistic terms by simply juxtaposing the names of Varus, Hermann and Hermann's wife, Thusnelda, at the base of a trail in the forest. . . . A network of spidery lines connects this bloody starting point to other names taken from later German history, thereby tying the German national heritage together into one comprehensible whole. The linear construct becomes a kind of chart of heredity, linking all parts inextricably (Rosenthal, 1987: 49).

I see the strange, weird forest, the setting of so many of Kiefer's paintings, as portraying the particular German biology. In one of his seminars, Jung said that the unconscious of the German race is very strong.[9] *Varus* conveys the feeling of a strong and wild unconscious and a nature that, in its fight against an alien force, remained uncontaminated. As a consequence,

Germany, geographically and psychologically, was not pervaded by the Roman civilization, which formed the matrix of European culture.

We have seen how Kiefer's creativity combines mythology and history, exploring the archetypal forms behind a people's historical behavior. His work is imaginatively enriching and challenging to a psychologist interested in studying the psyche from the same viewpoint of archetypal forms and historical complexes.

Continuing the historical theme, Kiefer produced several works entitled *Ways of Worldly Wisdom,* where he developed the ideas he first expressed in *Varus*. I shall discuss only one of these works—*Ways of Worldly Wisdom,* 1976–77 (page 49). The setting is the eerie Teutoberg forest, associated with the Battle of Arminius and with the Wotanic nature of the Germans. The historic heads are painted looming out of this ghostly petrified forest. One could say that the faces and names, caught among the roots of the trees themselves, are representatives of the bulk of German knowledge and culture. The painting can be viewed as depicting a historical web, a pictorial expression of the German historical complexes in which, at the lower left, is included the head of a dead German soldier. In the center of the painting there is a forest fire; the flames look as if they are licking the tree trunks. Fire appears in many of Kiefer's works; for him both forest and fire would seem to have a strong symbolic association with the German nature and history.

Arrogant German philosophy had dominated Western thought, but, "after the catastrophe," it became questionable. Obviously there was something wrong with the German *Bildung,* its academy and philosophy. Kiefer depicts the unreality and inflation embedded in the German tradition of knowledge. It was a knowledge that pretended to be well out of the forest and a contributor to universal enlightenment, but Kiefer places all those representative heads as firmly connected to their Wotanic roots. The vision brought to this painting moves us to reflect on those representatives of the German academy as being possessed by the same demonic forces that impelled Germany into the catastrophe. Kiefer's pictorial reflections make for a synthesis of the German nature and history, and the disastrous outcome reflected in the head of the dead German soldier. Undoubtedly this work gives a new turn to the genre of historical painting. Kiefer describes the depth and complexity of history in its connection to nature. His vision provides an extraordinary level of reflection.

In his testimony to the tragedy of the Spanish Civil War, *Guernica,* Picasso expressed his emotional outrage and suffering through the Spanish passion for the bull and horse. He used also the dead soldier as an expression of the destructive stupidity of war. While *Guernica* too has fiery symbolism and transmits strong emotions, Kiefer

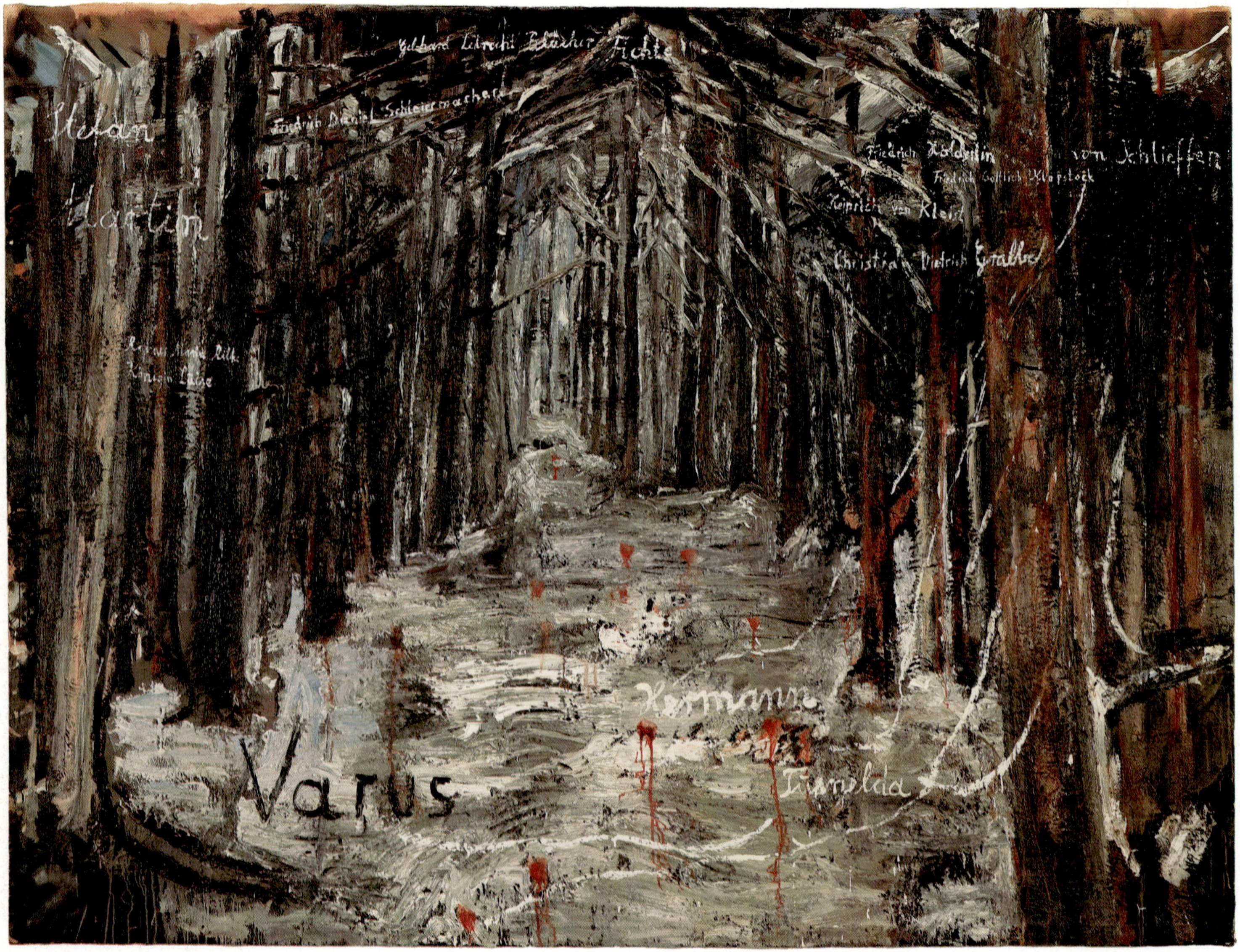
Gebhard Leberecht Blücher
Fichte
Stefan
Martin
von Schlieffen
Hermann
Varus

**Varus,** 1976

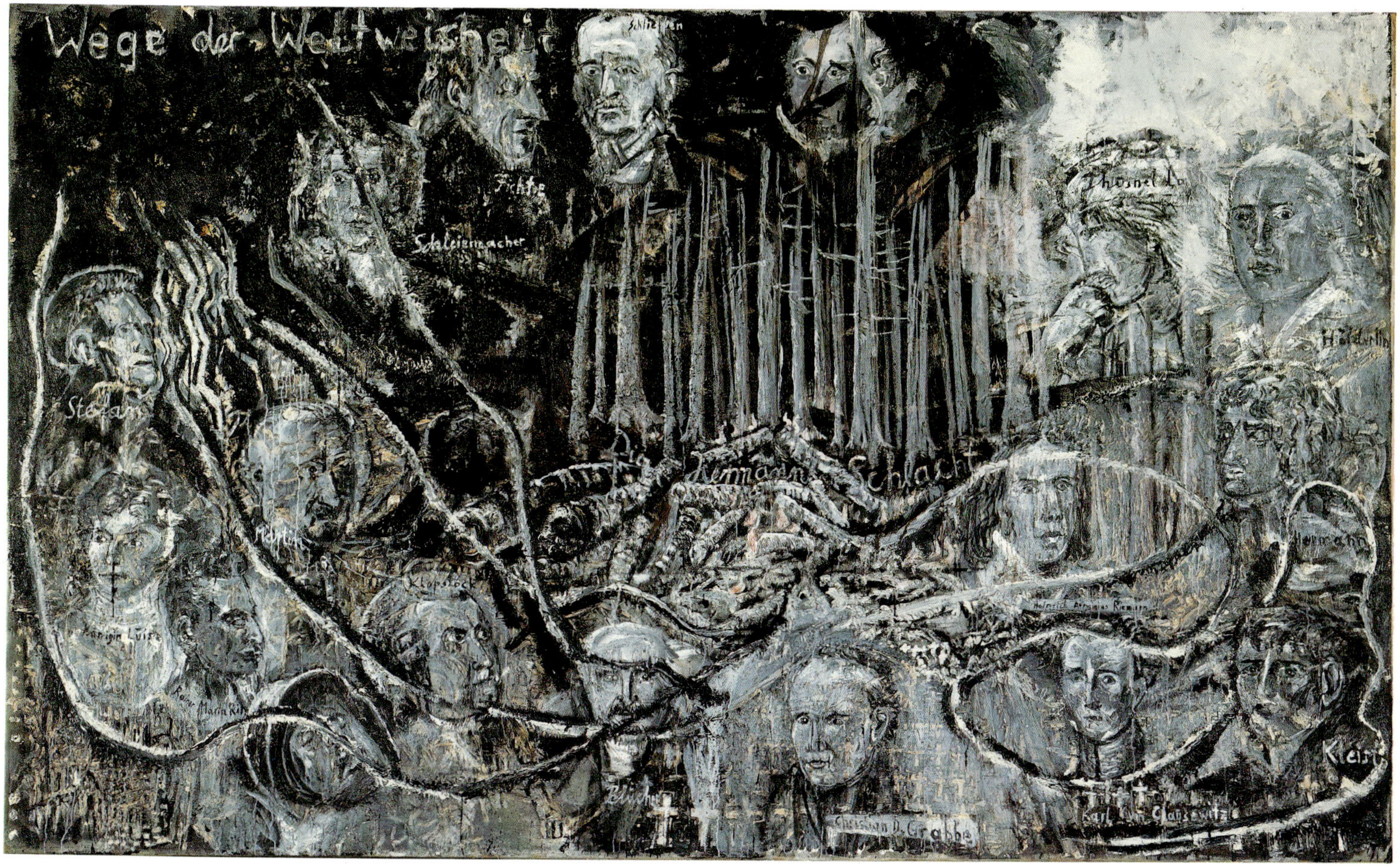


**Ways of Worldly Wisdom,** 1976–77

represents history in a more didactic way, as an unprecedented failure.

Just as we have seen that Kiefer's works on Germanic mythological themes are thought-provoking, so he produces a similar effect when he tackles Christian themes. It is with his reflections on Western civilization that we begin to move more deeply into the psychology of "after the catastrophe." The catastrophe opened up a new stratum of psychological reality. Religious and spiritual values were unable to contain the overwhelming forces that brought it about. One has to ask whether the onesidedness of these values, like that of the German intellect, was not at the core of the catastrophe, for such a perspective made for a total unawareness of the shadow.

The catastrophe exposed, in a traumatic way, the most inferior stratum in human nature. To confront such a stratum in our nature demands an awareness of the inferior psychopathic shadow and moreover, an acceptance of the constant fight with it. In Germany this shadow was hidden by a one-sided psychology, which included fairy tales, intellectual and philosophical inflations and ideologies, as well as the dreams of the generals and heroes. When Kiefer moves his pictorial reflections toward Christian themes, he complements Jung's view of the collapse of spiritual values in Western culture.

The striking painting *Father, Son, Holy Ghost,* 1973 (page 52), is Kiefer's rendering of Western culture's spiritual and religious tradition. It is a diptych of two canvases, the lower depicting another uncanny forest: the sap of life has dried up and all that remains are bare, aggressive, spiky branches. The pink trees give a strange quality to the work. The upper zone is a wooden room, another of Kiefer's favorite settings. The painting reflects the Christian Trinity through the graphic image of three transparent chairs—or the outline of three chairs—occupied by flames. Kiefer, who attempts to deal with his country's history and the extremity of religion's failure, forces us to re-assess the profound changes that have taken place in the Western spiritual tradition in times of "after the catastrophe."

This provocative painting can be viewed from the angle of alchemical symbolism. Outside, through the windows, we see snow. Inside, we see fire. Kiefer has an affinity to the opposites of hot and cold, as we saw in his book *Erotik im Fernen Osten oder: Transition from cool to warm.* Cold outside and heat inside have been connected to fever by the Jungian psychosomatist Alfred Ziegler:

> Alchemy, too, has found symbols for our existence in the contrasts of temperature: Boschius's emblem shows the Mount Etna volcano to be a massive, frozen block ablaze with flames. A meditative contemplation of such a paradoxical *Philosophem* best

illustrates our analytical concern with a syndrome like fever (1983: 152).

From the perspective of alchemy, fire acquires a specific psychological dynamism. Following Ziegler, the fire in this painting seems to point to a psychosomatic condition in relation to the Father, Son, and Holy Ghost. Kiefer would seem to be implying that the central dogma of Christianity is in a feverish condition and possibly in an alchemical process of transformation. Nevertheless, we can sense that the meaning of the Father, Son, and Holy Ghost has obviously faded in the course of history, especially since the catastrophe. It is here that Kiefer gives us a lesson in modern alchemy. We know that the opus of the medieval alchemist was, among other things, a way of assimilating religious symbolism, so rigidly dogmatized by the Christian Church, into an individual context. Kiefer's painting revivifies the alchemist's art by putting a timeless doctrine into a historical perspective.

We have seen that from Kiefer's first painting of a German mythological theme—*Nothung*—the father/son relationship has been present. He brings two traditions in relation to the father/son archetype: the Teutonic, which in the sense of a psychological inheritance could be seen as the autochthonous religion of the blood, and the more universal Christian dogma of the Father, Son, and Holy Ghost. Kiefer's imagery suggests that these two religious levels, the autochthonous and the Christian, are deeply conflictive in the German psyche, and we are moved to consider the complexity of these two levels in the German psychology. The painting itself shows the two levels in a striking imagery: the autochthonous German psyche, symbolized by the forest, holding the superstructure of the wooden attic in which is placed the Christian dogma of the Trinity. But if we see this only as a religious conflict, then we miss the level of biological ethnicity. The father/son relationship of Wotan and Siegfried, a specific mythological inheritance of the German people, is in conflict with the Christian dogma. Kiefer can only forge in his soul this complex and delicate issue.

Three years later, in *Faith, Hope, Love,* 1976 (page 53), Kiefer furthers his reflections concerning Christianity. He depicts the three Christian virtues as three petrified tree trunks growing out of a painter's palette. The trees are barren, with horizontal, black, spiky branches, conveying an unsettling deadness. Is Kiefer suggesting that individual creative imagination no longer functions with the collective values of the Christian virtues? The shocking color of the trees, their tormented shape, as well as the inscriptions of the virtues on the tree trunks, show Kiefer's artistic resources: he uses modern expressionism and conceptualism to hold his inner conflict in relation to the three theological virtues and his creative soul.

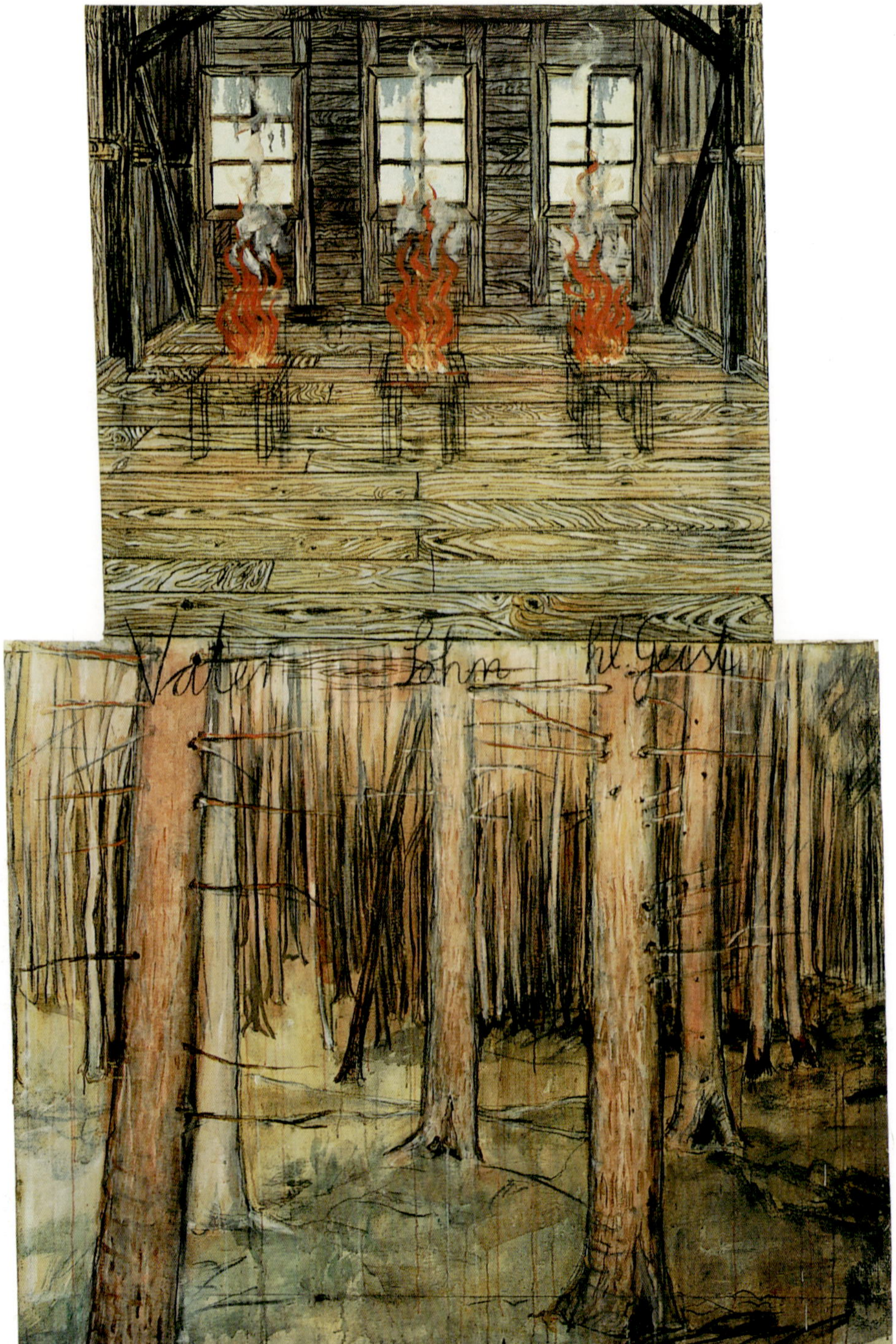


**Father, Son, Holy Ghost**
1973

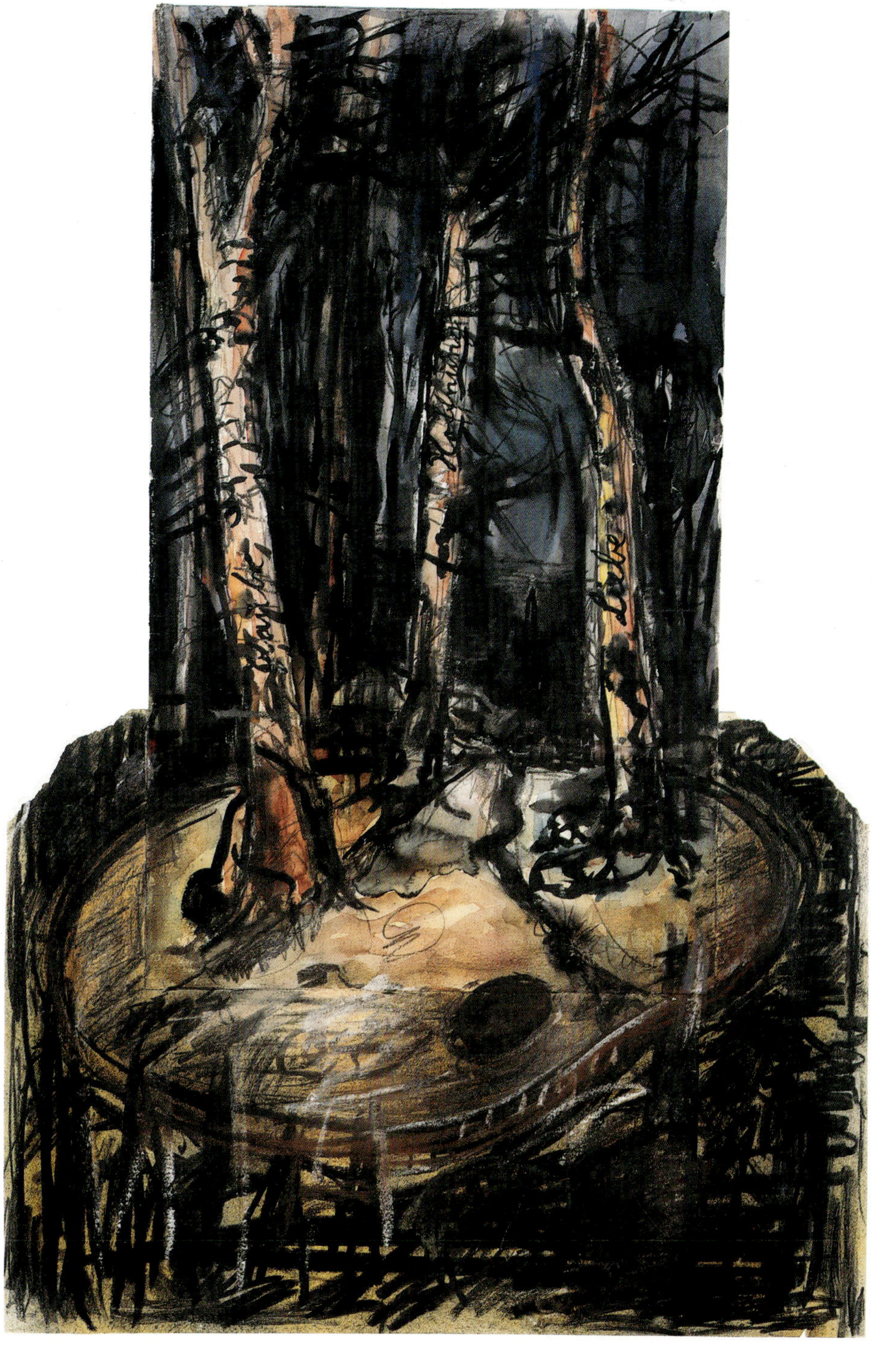

**Faith, Hope, Love**
1976

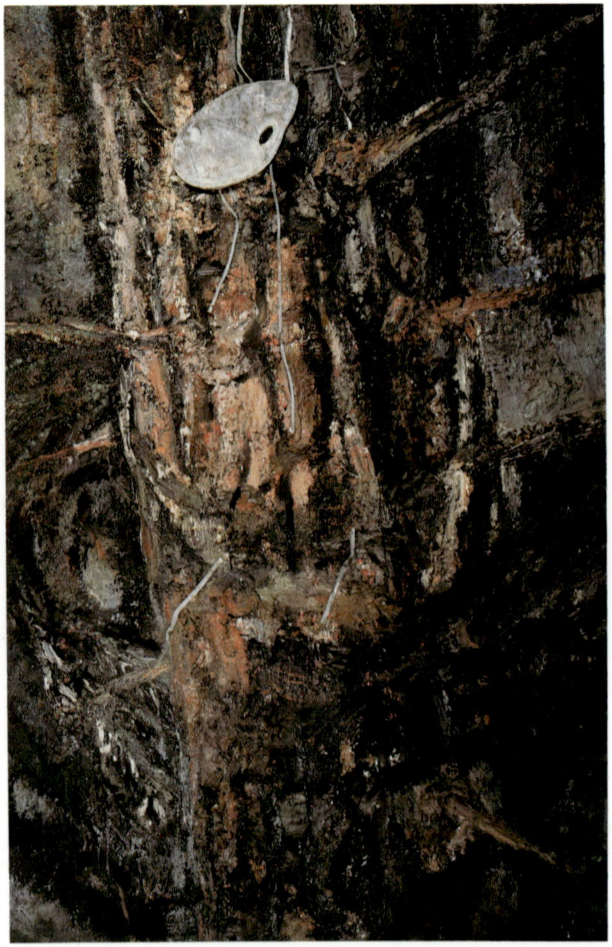

**Tree with Palette**
1977

As *Father, Son, Holy Ghost,* this work can also be viewed from the medieval alchemical imagination, but for this we need to have an idea of the old alchemical treatises on the philosophical tree. Jung (CW13, 304ff) worked out the symbolism of the tree, first through patients' tree-paintings showing both their psychological conflicts and therapeutical possibilities, and then through alchemical treatises, including those of Jodocus Greverus, Gerhard Dorn, and Petrus Bonus of Ferrara. In Kiefer's modern imagination, the philosophical tree now grows out of the painter's palette and includes the collective, historical, and religious complexes around the three theological virtues of Faith, Hope, and Love. The painting can be seen to express a serious collective disturbance in relation to the fundamental values of Christianity. Kiefer's receptive soul catches here a historical reality: the trees of Western religious life are now tormented, petrified, or lifeless, according to each one's subjective view, for *Faith, Hope, Love* invites many readings and emotional reactions.

That "The fourfold Mercurius is also the tree or its *spiritus vegetativus*" (CW13: 360) is relevant to this painting. There is a kinship between Hermes/Mercurius and the tree. This mercurial aspect was present in the treatises of the alchemists, as well as in Jung's interpretation of the philosophical tree and its therapeutic application. It is a thought-provoking line, especially in regard to the appearance of alchemy in modern psychotherapy. The *spiritus vegetativus* points to the neuro-vegetative system, giving us an idea of the depths from which Kiefer's painting emerged. I consider there to be abundant evidence to back this view, namely the many paintings of Kiefer in which strange forests appear, with the same strong organic quality.

In his dream seminars, Jung suggested that dreams might come from the neuro-vegetative system. Kiefer's painting conveys a dream-like imagination as a way of giving an answer to the inner tension created by the three theological virtues. There is an even more striking example of this connection in *Tree with Palette,* 1977 (page 54), in which we see a section of a tree trunk to which a tiny palette is attached. One feels how Kiefer's nature rejoiced in giving to the bark of the tree such a beautiful patina. Rosenthal remarks on how the painting "exhibits a heightened sense of drama" (1987: 66).

Another way of approaching Kiefer's creativity would be through Jung's conception of the archetypal spectrum, spanning the ultraviolet, ascensional spiritual pole of the archetype to the infrared, instinctive biological pole (CW8: 414). Again, the spectrum of the archetypes is to be taken metaphorically, here as a way of referring to a part of human nature that always remains obscure. From this point of departure, we can say that Kiefer paints mostly from the infrared end of the archetype, and it is from this instinctive level that he reflects the symbols so central to Christianity.

Kiefer's explorations occur within a sound knowledge of the history of painting and the possibilities offered by continual advances in the visual arts. In the tradition of German art, paintings hint at the conflicts underlying the distortions of Expressionism, the strange forces that nourish his artistic heritage. We can psychologically assimilate the emotion from the way he seems to explore alchemy and the way he reflects Christian myth. Moreover, in such works as *Faith, Hope, Love* he gives an unexpected twist to religious painting, provoking reflection in an age in which religion has become in many ways the unreflective practice of repetitive dogmas.

Kiefer brings a very personal approach to Judaism, one that is neither moralistic nor guilt-making. He has evidently asked himself some searching questions concerning the horrifying history of the Germans and the Jews. In 1984 he made a trip to Israel that seems to have been another *peregrinatio,* this time in search of Jewish legends. His way of approaching Judaism involved an effort similar to his quest for the German mytho-poetical roots by making the trip to Norway. He was obviously very struck by the desert geography, as attested to in *Departure from Egypt,* 1984–85 (page 57). Just as he associated myth and landscape in *North Cape,* here Kiefer finds the setting for expressing his reflections on the theme of the Exodus in the dramatic concrete topography of the desert origins of the Jewish people.

A photograph of a desert was the starting point for *Departure from Egypt,* 1984–85. Although the border between the upper and the lower spheres is distinct,

> a painted cloud drips from the heavens, as if giving a sign to the inhabitants below, an allusion to the Exodus story, in which the God of Israel presents Himself to His people in a pillarlike cloud (Rosenthal, 1987: 121).

As Rosenthal explains, Kiefer depicts the Jews' connection to their Godhead, a connection that is central to their religion and way of life. Toynbee gives importance to the environment where the unique spirituality of the Jews was formed: "From the barren wilderness of the Judean desert, the Israelites wrested a spiritual intuition of the unity and omnipotence of God" (1979: 80). *Departure from Egypt* brings a pictorial synthesis of the most characteristic trait of the Jewish people and their God. Kiefer's magnificent conception conveys the restlessness and energy required for traveling through the desert and, in a wider sense, through the world where the Jewish people have had to adapt in a constant struggle for survival and their connection to their God, who dictated their religious laws and way life.

With great honesty, Kiefer goes straight to the most archaic Jewish legends and, through his treatment of a wide range of Jewish motifs, reflects a psychology in depth. Mark Rosenthal presents Kiefer's painting *The Red Sea,* 1984–85 (page 59):

> Kiefer brings the Exodus tale into a German context in *The Red Sea,* 1984–85. The connection is forged by the carryover of the National Socialism bathtub from the Operation Sea Lion series. . . . The tub full of red liquid . . . links two biblical events, the first plague in Exodus, when Aaron turned water to blood with his rod, and Moses's parting and closing of the sea with his staff. . . . A glass plate like the one that held the chairs of the Trinity aloft appears above the earth holding a white "pillar of cloud" (1987: 127).

*The Red Sea* is another powerful conception. As stated by Rosenthal, Kiefer makes an unmistakable connection between the Exodus and Operation Sea Lion. He portrays the Red Sea motif in a way similar to his portrayal of the German generals planning their operation with boats in a bathtub. In a remarkable twist of imagination, Kiefer relates the German generals' fantasy of crossing the English Channel to the biblical fantasy of Moses's parting and crossing the Red Sea. In this case, the motif of the bathtub is used by Kiefer as a metaphor to link complexes that, though profoundly disturbing, are the source of psychic movement and creativity. In his *Departure from Egypt,* Kiefer shows an admirably profound intuition into the ascensional spirituality of the Jewish religious complex and its geographical cradle. In *The Red Sea* he connects to the archaic part of the complex, where magic is an important ingredient, which can only be approached through poetical and primitive thought. At the same time, is Kiefer implying that the Jewish psyche is stuck in repetitive complexes that no longer nourish it? In any event, it would

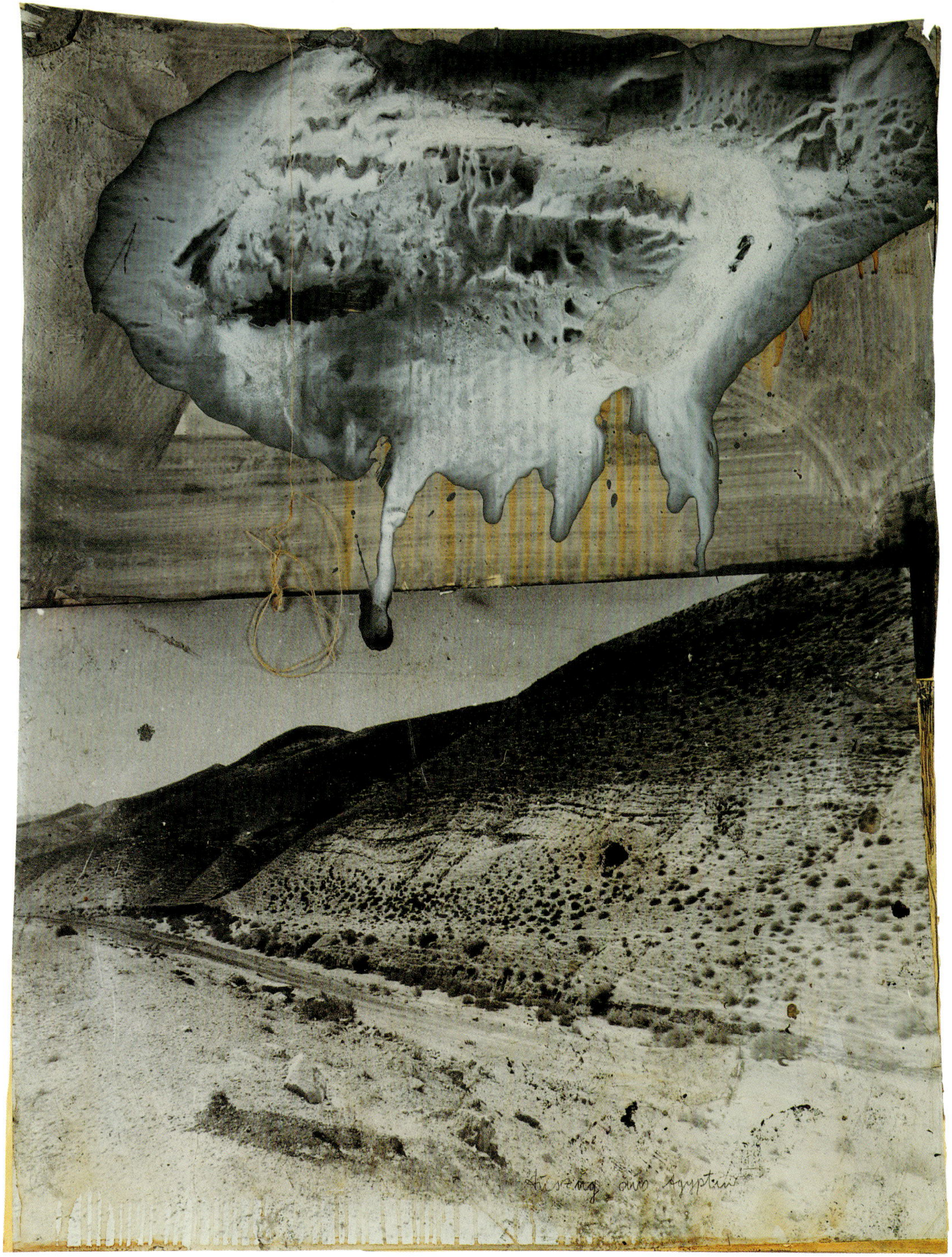

**Departure from Egypt**
1984–85

seem that he attempts to put aspects of the German and Jewish psyches into the same psychological vessel and, with this rendering of *The Red Sea,* makes a psychological symmetry out of the most absurd side of their joint psychologies. Or, as in *Operation Sea Lion,* he makes a symmetry with the stupidity that is concomitant with power. I consider that Kiefer, who as a German is suffering from a mammoth historical failure, cannot avoid his artistic curiosity in this respect, and so, through his art, questions and reflects the old Jewish complexes in relation to their present historical reality.

If Kiefer's conception of *The Red Sea* is a challenge, his conception of Jerusalem is very personal and moves our collective traditional imagination concerning the Holy City. The painting *Jerusalem,* 1986 (page 60), is an expressionist abstraction, elaborated with acrylic, emulsion, gold leaf, lead and two striking steel bars.

The abstraction of the painting and its title make me recall a personal memory of Jerusalem. One of the most important occasions at the Ninth International Congress of Analytical Psychology, held in Jerusalem in 1983, was a morning devoted to representatives of the three monotheistic religions—a Jewish scholar, a Catholic priest, and a Muslim imam—talking about the meaning of Jerusalem for their respective religions. All the Jungians present were enchanted with the three different views. A beatific spirit of tolerance floated in the crowd that morning. There was not the faintest allusion to the shadow and hatred that three monotheistic religions, living together in a city, must inevitably constellate. The attitude of all present was very far from the basic premise of Jungian psychology: to learn from the shadow. The myth of religious tolerance had everyone in its thrall and threw a smoke screen over the bloody history of the religions. But it is very difficult to learn from the shadow, as the history of Western culture attests.

In view of the history of the city, the religious conceptions of Jerusalem, psychologically speaking, are certainly products of a religious inflation. The image alone of a place where three monotheistic religions cohabit, where the psyche has to deal constantly with three exclusive religious systems seems to be an infernal image, difficult to match. Does not religion show its most destructive aspect in the inevitable, never-ending friction between the three faiths? Could it be said that, throughout its history, from the earliest times, when the Jewish people projected their fantasy onto the city, down to our own days, Jerusalem can be seen as a symbol precariously holding both religion and inferior psychopathy? We owe it to Jung's genius that religion was brought into the study of modern psychology. A religion is a vessel that can contain and heal the complexities and madness of human nature. It is within this Jungian legacy and according to the times in

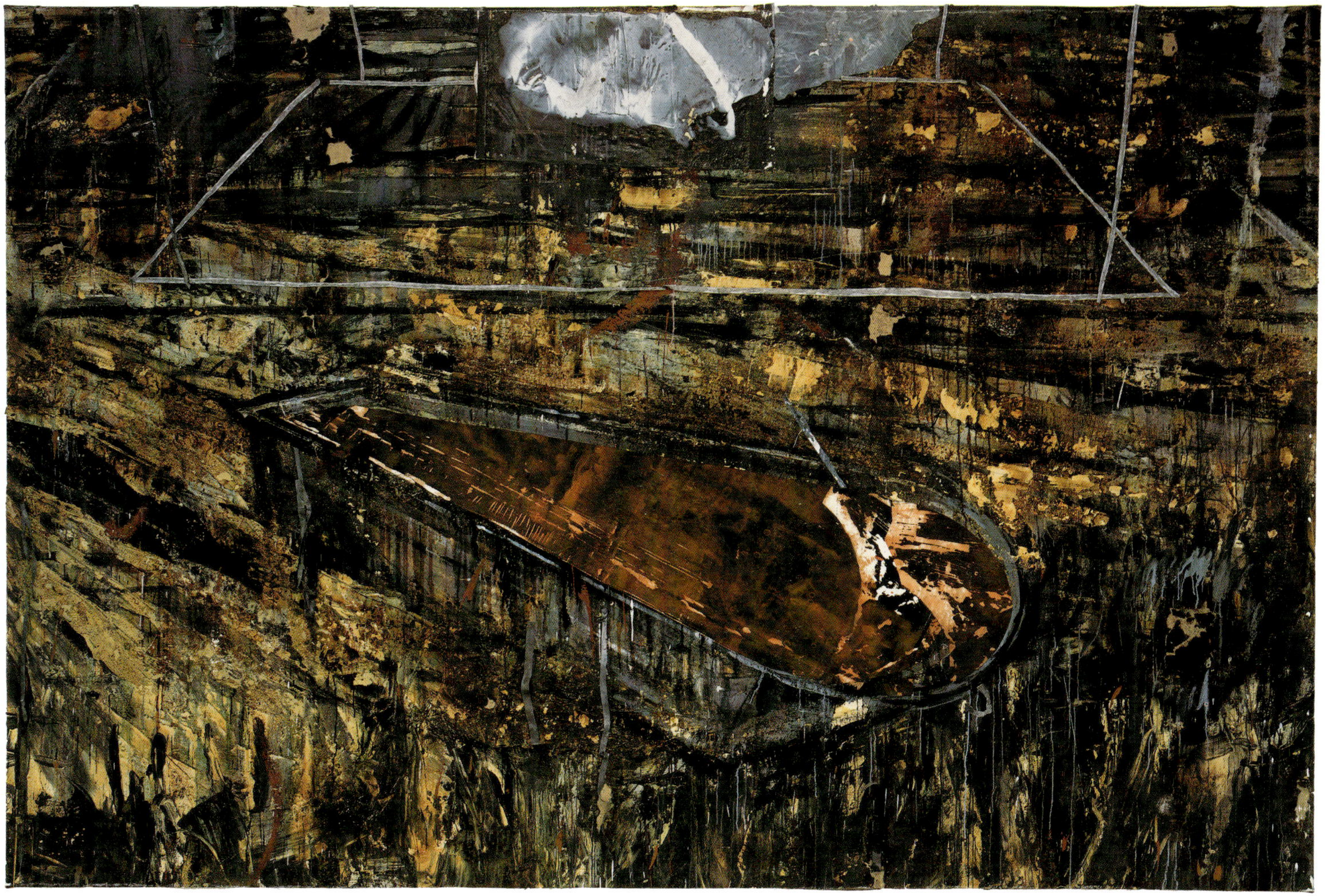

**The Red Sea,** 1984–85

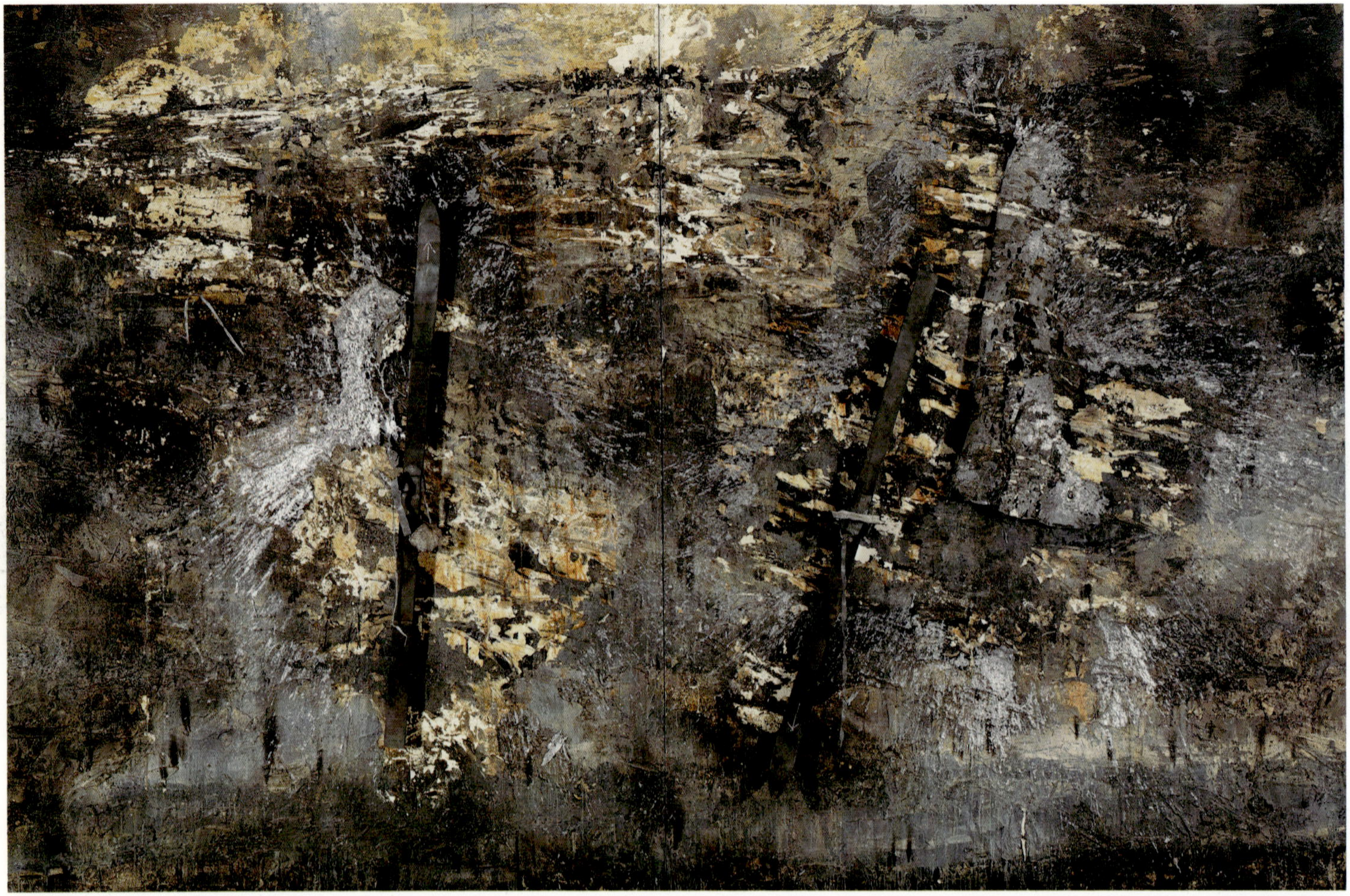

**Jerusalem,** 1986

which we are living—the times of "after the catastrophe"—that we can begin to bring some differentiation to psychology and religion. For we have to see that the individual psyche is one thing and religious systems are another. This might help us to adopt a less hypocritical attitude and become more aware of the shadow that the historical religions constellate.

It is possible to say that Kiefer's trip to Israel and his excursion into the Jewish legends—such as the Exodus, Aaron, the Miracle of the Serpents, Lilith, and, later, Kabbalistic themes such as the Seferoth and Emanation—were to fill his imagination with the essences of Judaism. The result was a series of marvelous paintings. It was the sort of mytho-historical regression in which Kiefer is so gifted: a step backward of millennia as a psychological preparation before tackling an image through which he moved into Jewish contemporary history and came closer to the forces that brought about the Holocaust.

When he discovered Paul Celan's great poem, "Death Fugue" (Celan, 1980), with the two lines "your golden hair Margarete / your ashen hair Shulamith," we can imagine that, in a flash of intuition, he saw a picture of the whole historical tragedy of the Germans and the Jews. It is to be noted that in 1981, well before his trip to Israel, Kiefer, was already immersed in Celan's poem. I would say that, cautiously, he started to move his imagination into the theme of Margarete, representing the German pole of the tragedy, in a painting called *Margarete,* 1981, where she is depicted as plants of straw with burning tips. Then, as the image became clearer, he painted *Your Golden Hair, Margarete,* 1981 (page 62), a direct reference to Celan's poem. A lock of her hair, depicted in straw, is superimposed over a barren countryside of furrows stretching to a far horizon.

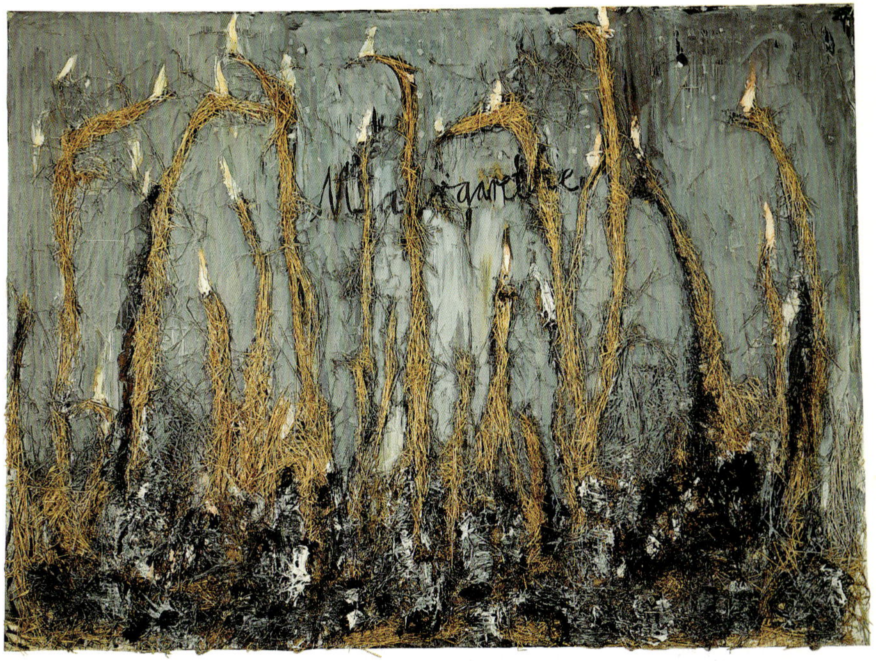

**Margarete,** 1981

It was now that Kiefer turned to the image of Shulamite (Sulamith), representing the Jewish pole, an image that would haunt him for a decade. In the frightening painting *Shulamite,* 1983 (page 63), Kiefer equates the woman at the center of the most beautiful poetry in Jewish literature—The Song of Songs—with a dark claustrophobic mili-

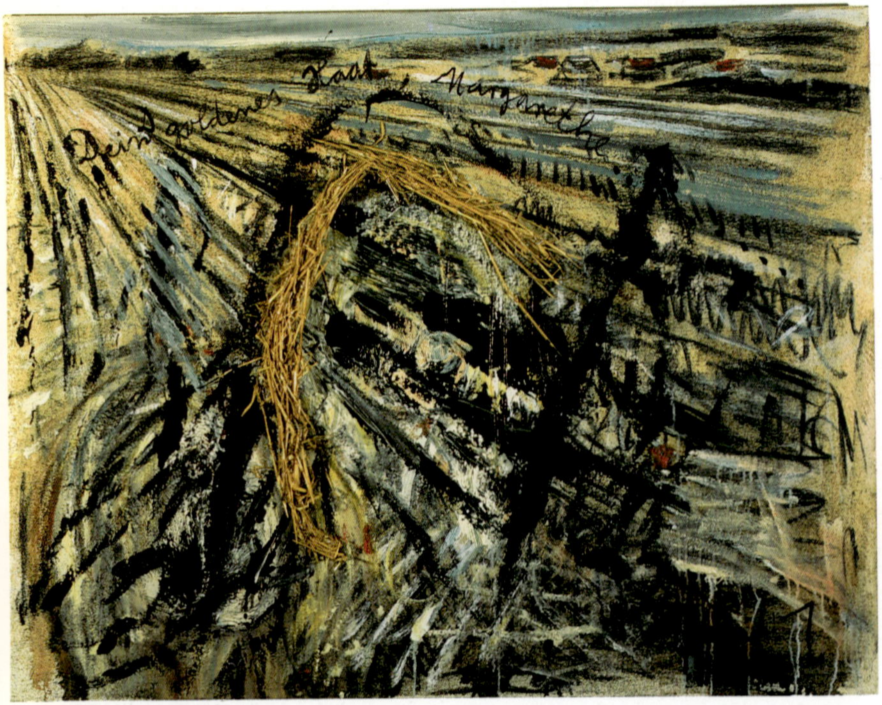

**Your Golden Hair, Margarete**
1981

tary castle. Shulamite, who we can say personifies the Jewish poetical soul, is depicted as a bunker. It is a mind-blowing conception indeed. The pictorial language is similar to that which Kiefer brings to German mythology, Christianity and history, and its emotional impact is as strong. For example, the claustrophobic brooding atmosphere of *Shulamite* has a psychological tension similar to that of such works as *Parsifal* or *Father, Son, Holy Ghost.* At the top left corner, Kiefer has written "Sulamith," taken from Celan's poem *Death Fugue.* Both the poet and the painter bring a vision of the historical transition of the Jewish poetical soul from Solomon's Song of Songs to a concentration camp. Kiefer seems to be showing that there is no space for the Jewish poetical soul to flower, it is imprisoned in a bunker.[10] Kiefer has made a very honest and symmetrical approach to Judaism.

Before moving further into the complexities expressed in Celan's "Death Fugue" and Kiefer's evident fascination with "your golden hair Margarete / your ashen hair Shulamith," it is important to have a picture of Celan's background and life.[11]

Paul Antschel (Celan) was born on November 23, 1920, in Czernowitz, the capital of Bukovina, a small region between the Rumanian Transylvania and Bessarabia, which belonged to the Austro-Hungarian Empire until the end of the Hapsburg monarchy in 1918. A few months before he was born, the region was incorporated into Rumania. It was what could be called a very ethnic region where many different races lived: Rumanians, Ruthenians, Germans, Jews, Armenians, Magyars, Poles, Lipovanes, and Hutsuls. In Czernowitz, the Jews comprised roughly half of the inhabitants. Culturally, they identified with the Germans, and German was the language at the University of Czernowitz. In a later recollection, Celan said: "The region from which I come . . . will be unfamiliar to most of you. It is the home of many of the Hassidic stories which Martin Buber has retold in German. It was . . . a landscape where both people and books lived" (Colin, 1991: 4).

Paul Antschel was the only son of Leo Antschel-

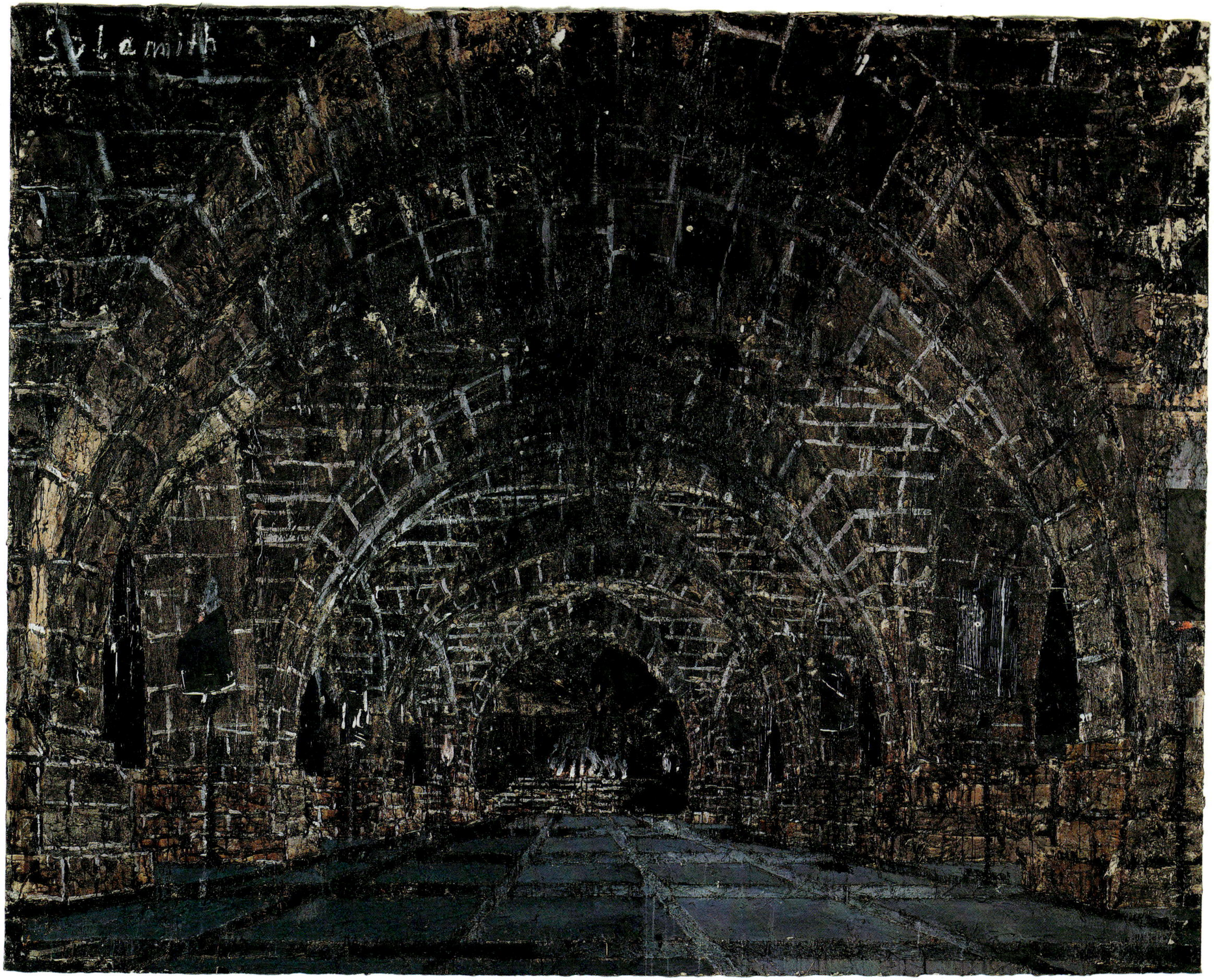


**Shulamite,** 1983

Teitler, a construction technician and salesman, and Friederike Schrager, who came from a merchant family. His mother spoke high German (though the family spoke Yiddish together). She considered herself to be assimilated to the German culture, whereas his father dreamed of emigrating to Palestine. Perhaps he had an intuition of what was to come. "The tension between his [Paul's] German and Jewish legacies stigmatized his youth" (Colin, 1991: xiii). In 1933, when German anti-Semitism spread to a great part of Europe, the difficult years started for Celan. Nevertheless, at a young age, in 1934–35, Paul took a course in the German language and then read Lessing, Goethe, Schiller, Kleist, Hölderlin and Rilke. In choosing literature for his studies, he learned Greek, Latin, and French and read Corneille, Racine, Verlaine, and Rimbaud.

After the Nonaggression Pact between Hitler and Stalin in 1939, Bukovina was invaded by the Russians and Communism was imposed. On May 13, 1941, the Russians deported to Siberia four thousand "unreliable" citizens, three quarters of whom were Jews. On May 22, Hitler invaded the U.S.S.R., and on July 5, German troops entered Czernowitz, killing all the people who had collaborated with the Russians. The next day, the S.S. arrived with precise orders to exterminate all Jews. The synagogue was burned on July 7 and Jews were declared to be beyond the law for seventy-two hours, during which time 682 Jews were exterminated and, according to a report sent to Berlin by S.S. Brigadier General Ohlendorf, there were three thousand more by the end of August.

> Celan recognized the looming danger. Though he implored his parents to leave their house and go into hiding as he did, they would not listen to him. After an argument with his father, Antschel left home; upon his return the next day, he found that his parents had been deported to Transnistria. Later, the terrifying news reached him: his father had died of typhoid and his mother had been shot dead. Antschel, guilt-ridden, miraculously escaped deportation to the death camp, but he was sent to forced labor, to shovel stones and dig roads. "I have seen life exchanged for utmost bitterness," wrote Antschel from the Roumanian labor detachment "Tabaresti" (in Buzau, Southern Moldavia) on 2 August 1942 (Colin, 1991: xiv).

In spite of shock, grief and guilt, Paul managed to survive the years of the German occupation, staying in Czernowitz until April 1945. It was poetry that kept him alive. Colin gives a beautiful image of survival through poetry under extreme conditions:

> The holocaust tragically intensified the bond between these Jewish poets from the Bukovina who continued to write in their native tongue within the ghetto and the concentration camps. Poems could be composed with limited writing materials on small pieces of paper and could be hidden easily. Set against the chaos and cruelty of reality, the integrity of poetry gave these

> deportees strength and purpose. Some of their texts make few direct references to the war and the camps, but speak of love and reminiscences of happier times. Other poems, however, describe the murders, thus acquiring the significance of historical documents (1991: 22).

After the war, Paul Celan eventually settled in Paris (1948–70), where he created some of his major works (Colin, 1991: xvi). He studied German literature there and, after graduating in 1950, taught German at the École Normale Supérieure. He married the graphic artist Gisèle Lestrange in 1952. Their first son, François, died; their second son, Eric, was born in 1955. The year of his marriage he published the book of poems he considered to be his first: *Mohn und Gedachtnis*. It included "Death Fugue," which had been published earlier in Vienna, and other new ones. From then on, Paul Celan wrote and published his works, receiving the most important and prestigious German literary prizes. In April 1970, at less than fifty years of age, he committed suicide by throwing himself into the Seine. His poems are recognized as some of the greatest works of this century in the German language.

There are three aspects in this very reduced biographical note on Celan that capture my attention. First, the cultural differences between his father and mother, mirroring two attitudes that have been present throughout the history of the Jewish Diaspora—the Zealotism of the father, with his fantasy of going to Palestine, and the assimilation of the mother to the German culture, proud of her knowledge of its language and literature. These differences created a tension in the young Paul and formed his psychology. However, it was a conflict that pushed him into the study of languages and literature, enriching an already gifted poetical soul. Celan's attraction to and assimilation of the German culture and his Jewishness were in a conflict from the beginning, a conflict exacerbated by the Holocaust. There was the later dilemma of writing in both "the mother's tongue and the murderer's tongue" (Colin, 1991: xvii).

Secondly, Celan remembered the Bukovina as a paradise where men and books lived; this was true on a poetical level. Czernowitz was undoubtedly an extraordinary place where a tremendous literary movement happened, as is attested to by many scholars. Amy Colin's book on Celan brings a fascinating picture of this movement. However, the historical reality was that of a geographical pocket in which many ethnicities lived together in a shadow conflict. Later, under the Nazi occupation, this became a historical inferno. I would say that such ethnic frictions sharpened Celan's sensitivity to the ethnic shadow:

> "Well, regarding anti-Semitism in our school, I could write a book three hundred pages thick," observed Antschel in 1934, when confronted with the growing racism of his Roumanian teachers (Colin, 1991: xiv).

Thirdly, I am fascinated with how Celan survived the Holocaust. It seems to me the hermetic side of his nature saved him during those horrifying years, the same hermetic nature that made a jigsaw puzzle of his poems for the literary critics and scholars on Jewish Holocaust literature.

Paul Celan's suffering was expressed in his poetry, above all in the great poem "Death Fugue":

> Black milk of daybreak we drink it at sundown
> we drink it at noon in the morning we drink it at night
> we drink and we drink it
> we dig a grave in the breezes there one lies unconfined
> A man lives in the house he plays with the serpents he writes
> he writes when dusk falls to Germany your golden hair
>     Margarete
> he writes it and steps out of doors and the stars are flashing he
>     whistles his pack out
> he whistles his Jews out in earth has them dig for a grave
> he commands us strike up for the dance
>
> Black milk of daybreak we drink you at night
> we drink in the morning at noon we drink you at sundown
> we drink and we drink you
> A man lives in the house he plays with the serpents he writes
> he writes when dusk falls to Germany your golden hair
>     Margarete
> your ashen hair Shulamith we dig a grave in the breezes there
>     one lies unconfined.
>
> He calls out jab deeper into the earth you lot you others sing now
>     and play
> he grabs at the iron in his belt he waves it his eyes are blue
> jab deeper you lot with your spades you others play on for the
>     dance
>
> Black milk of daybreak we drink you at night
> we drink you at noon in the morning we drink you at sundown
> we drink and we drink you
> a man lives in the house your golden hair Margarete
> your ashen hair Shulamith he plays with the serpents
> He calls out more sweetly play death death is a master from
>     Germany
> he calls out more darkly now stroke your strings then as smoke
>     you will rise into air
> then a grave you will have in the clouds there one lies unconfined
>
> Black milk of daybreak we drink you at night
> we drink you at noon death is a master from Germany
> we drink you at sundown and in the morning we drink and we
>     drink you
> death is a master from Germany his eyes are blue
> he strikes you with leaden bullets his aim is true
> a man lives in the house your golden hair Margarete
> he sets his pack on to us he grants us a grave in the air
> he plays with the serpents and daydreams death is a master from
>     Germany
>
> your golden hair Margarete
> your ashen hair Shulamith
>
> (1980: 50–53)

The opening words of the poem, "black milk of daybreak," express a suffering without parallel, and the lines "he whistles his Jews out in earth has them dig for a grave / he commands us strike up for the dance" is an image of evil made into poetry. Out of this suffering and incomparable vision of evil came the evocative lines that so affected Kiefer: "your golden hair Margarete / your ashen hair Shulamith."

Margarete and Shulamith are taken from the great literature of the past, from Goethe and Solomon respectively, yet, in Celan's hands, they conjure up vividly the origins of the conflict between the Germans and the Jews and its diabolical consequences. With the golden and ashen hair, Celan moves the image out of a poetic description to reveal the ethnic differences between Margarete and Shulamith, thus touching on the shadow sources of the tragedy. It is far more telling than the usual view of victim and victimizer. These two lines are a condensation of Paul Celan's individual poetic view of the history of the Germans and the Jews, with all its suffering and evil. The ashen hair of Shulamith tells us of an ethnicity at the core of the Jewish soul, and, taking this a step further, we begin to suspect that, at bottom, the Jewish soul suffers not only from its "original" guilt but also from ethnic shame.

Following Jung, we can say that Margarete and Shulamith are two anima figures for Paul Celan, two animas in ethnic opposition. When considering the unbearable suffering of Paul Celan and the tragic end of his life, I would risk the conjecture that the tension engendered by these two animas cannot be omitted, even though Celan could be taken as a model for an assimilated Jew. To conceive of Margarete and Shulamith as two inner anima figures in ethnic conflict and, at the same time, in opposition to a strong Jewish consciousness, is a challenge for the student of depth psychology.

In reality, we know very little about Jewish psychology, but it seems that for the Jews psychology and religion are one and the same, so they experience life through a collective consciousness, rooted in guilt. Such a psychology evidently had to do with Jung's observation of the Jews "strong" consciousness and "weak" unconscious (cf., note 9). For instance, Franz Kafka's psychology has been of tremendous interest, not only from the literary (he turned Jewish guilt into a unique art), but also from the Judaic point of view. Gershom Scholem, the great Jewish scholar on the Kabbala and Jewish mysticism notes that Kafka had deep roots in the tradition of Jewish mysticism (1965: 12). But Amy Colin brings a more relevant psychological description of Kafka when she cites Marthe Robert in her book *Franz Kafka's Loneliness,* where Kafka is described as an "assimilated Jew, anti-Jewish Jew, anti-Zionist, Zionist, believer, atheist—Kafka was indeed all of these at different times in his development, sometimes all at once" (1991: xxii). Colin goes on to observe: "Some of these characteristics could hardly apply to Celan—but the idea of a multiple identity is valid for Celan as well." We become aware of such a psychology through great Jewish artists like Kafka and Celan, whose individual necessity

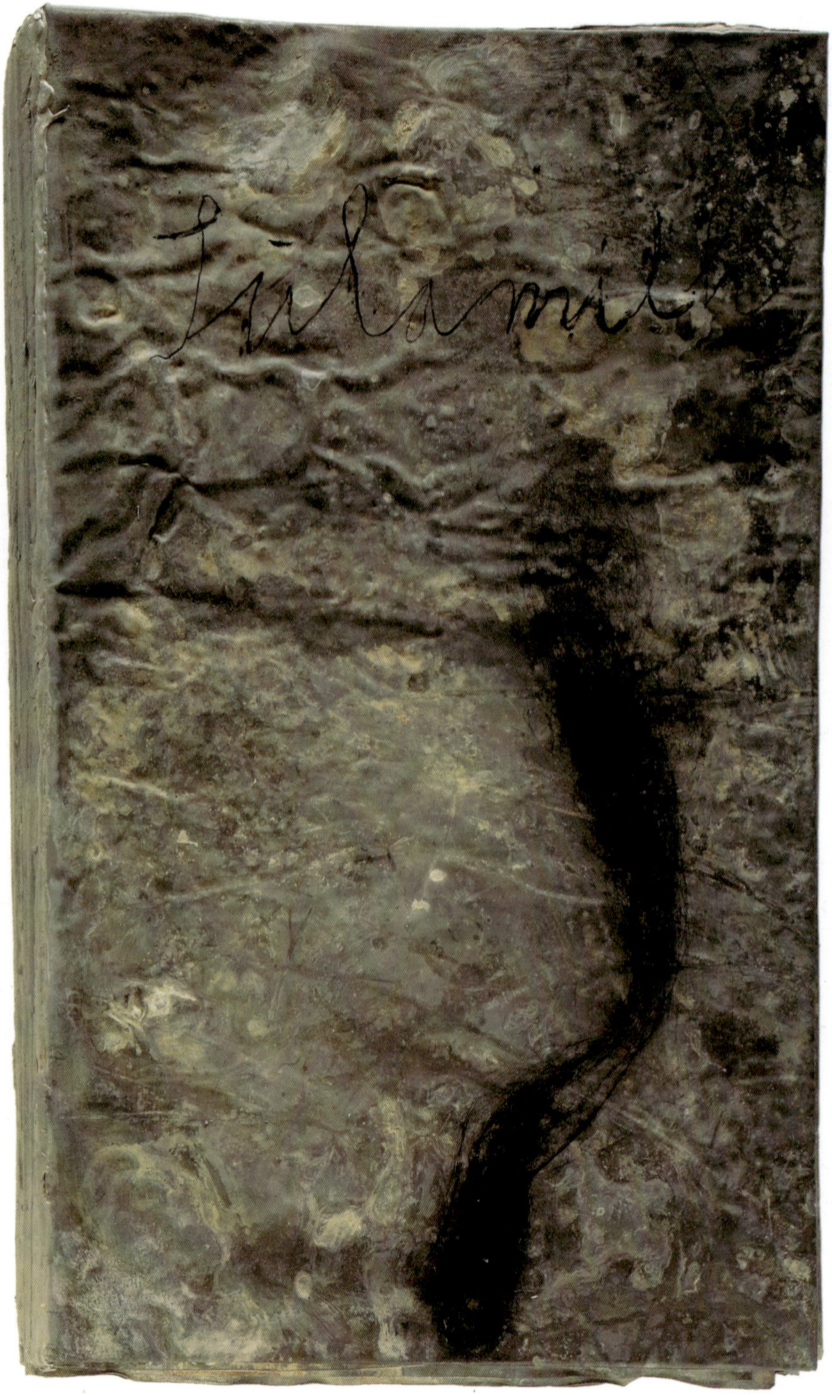


**Shulamith**
1990

breaks through the barriers of that strong collective consciousness. It is through their work that we catch a glimpse of what Jewish psychology might be, and it is a psychology that can be observed in a great number of cultured Jews.

It is interesting to note another feature of Jewish psychology. Jung records that Freud said to him, "My dear Jung, promise me never to abandon the sexual theory. That is the most essential thing of all. You see, we must make a dogma of it, an unshakable bulwark" (1963: 147). Freud's attitude is a clear example of totalitarianism. One sees also that totalitarianism and dogmatic reduction go together: sexuality reducing the wealth of the imagination and, moreover, blocking the possibility to learn from the shadow. However, I do not find this aspect as exciting as the picture of Kafka's psychology brought by Robert. One wonders if any of the complex psychology so beautifully expressed by Kafka and Celan, whose art presumably came from a weak unconscious, has been transferred to a conception of a modern Jewish psychology. Here again art teaches more than psychology. When a great poet like Paul Celan, under the pressure of a terrible suffering, dredges up from his poetical soul a poem like "Death Fugue," with the line "your ashen hair Shulamith," a line that goes to the root of Judaism, it can be welcomed as a great psychological event.

In the world of art, there has always been a strong connection between painters and poets, each stimulating the other. Of the many encounters between a painter and a poet, one of the most dramatic is that of Anselm Kiefer and Paul Celan through the poem "Death Fugue." Furthermore, one has to recognize that it is difficult to find an example in the history of art to come up to that of Anselm Kiefer in his historical task of carrying in his own soul Paul Celan's "Death Fugue," a poem that evokes the most terrible and destructive shadow of his own German people and, at the same time, expresses the Jewish ethnic shadow. In Germany before Hitler, the Jewish Diaspora was driven by an unreflective love for the German culture, leading to the illusion of being assimilated. But now we have to recognize that it was the fantasy of assimilation to a shadow-culture with Wotanic roots and its own peculiar biology. Also we have to consider that this notion of Jewish assimilation hit the Germans at just that ethnic biological level. Kiefer's creativity seems to have reached deeply into the Jewish soul and, in trying to penetrate the mystery of Jewish psychology, he measures up to Paul Celan's imagery of it.



In 1990, a decade later, evidently still under the impact of "Death Fugue," Kiefer produced two books with the theme of Shulamith. This time the books, both called *Shulamith* (pages 68, 70–72), are made of soldered lead and women's hair. The bunches and locks of hair on the texture of the

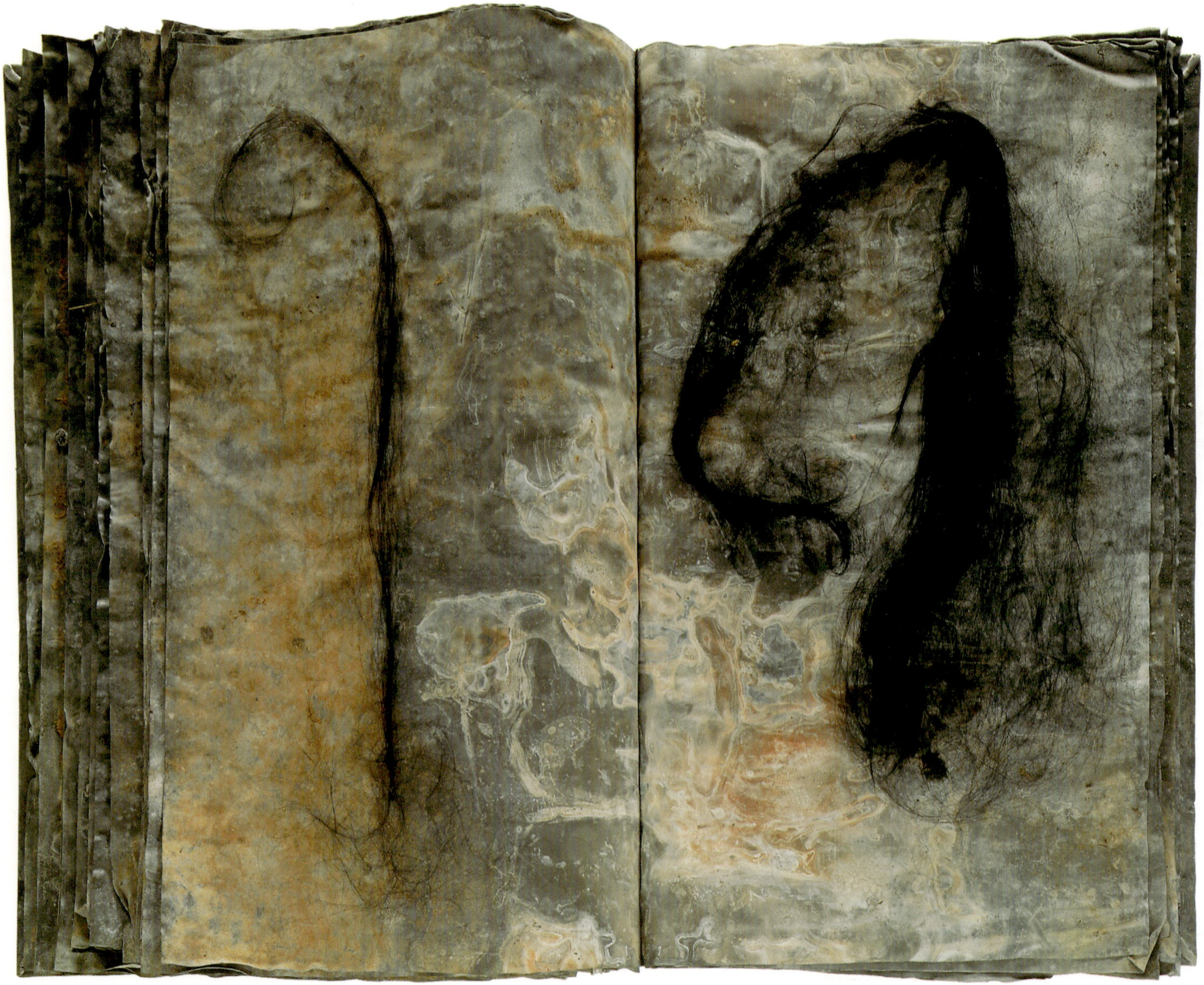

**Shulamith,** 1990

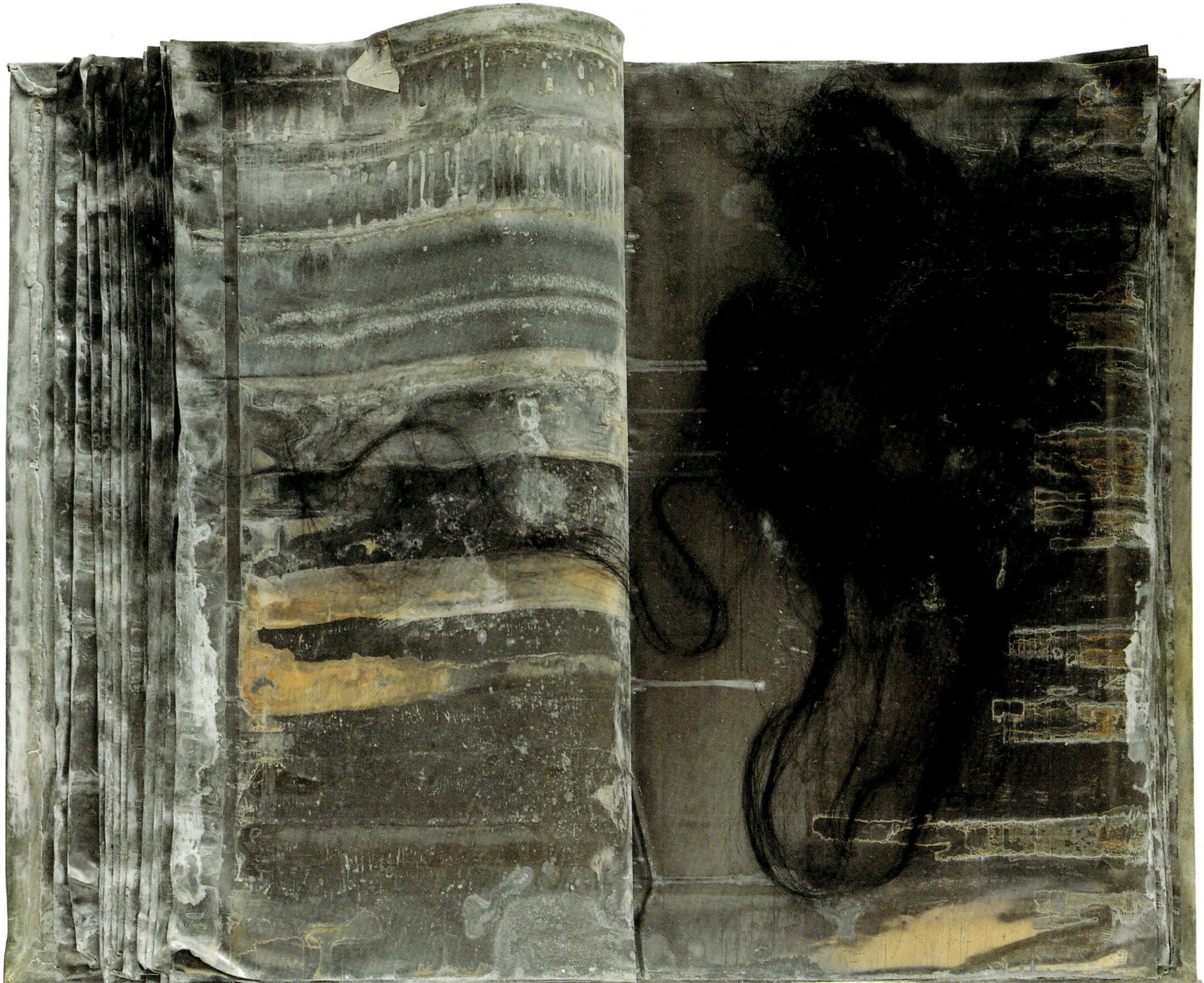

**Shulamith,** 1990

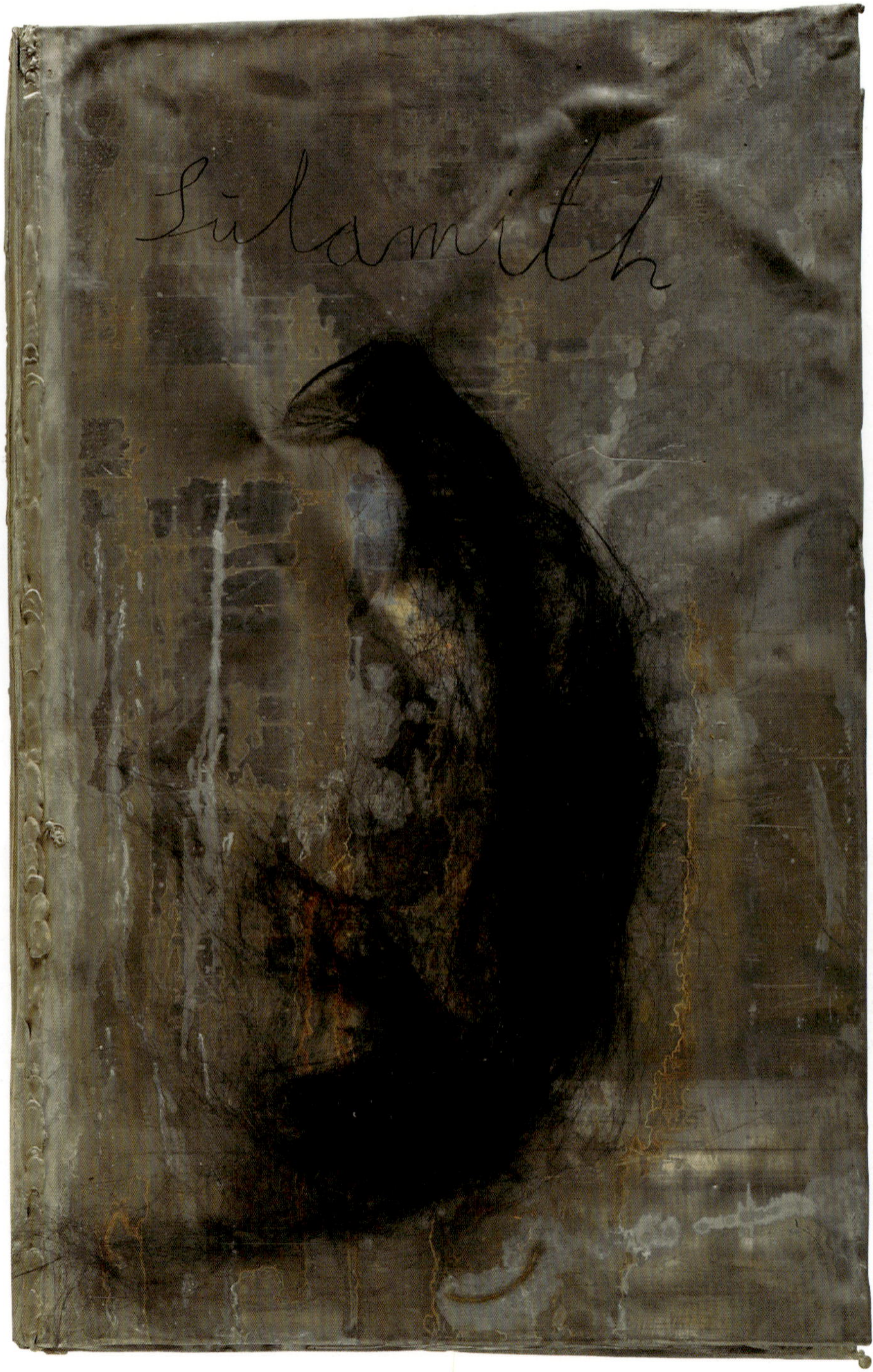


**Shulamith**
1990

lead produce a most uncomfortable effect; they transmit the horror of a concentration camp. They even activate our senses, above all our sense of smell: we can "smell" the concentration camp and the ovens. In creating this effect, Kiefer makes an important psychological connection. Hell is imagined through the sense of smell in Saint Ignatius of Loyola's *Spiritual Exercises*. It seems to me that Ignatius's conception was backed by the medieval alchemical imagination that considered hell to be evoked through the smell of sulphur. The patina of Kiefer's lead pages has a corrosive, sulphuric aspect, bringing to mind this alchemical association, but, at the same time, lending the pages a strange beauty. Here Kiefer shows us again that art is the *via regia* for reflecting horror.

The fact that Kiefer has continued to make books on Shulamith suggests that his soul has been submerged to the point of obsession with the historical complexes contained in the theme. Previously, I discussed Margarete and Shulamith as conflictive animas in Paul Celan. Now, I would like to ask: What is happening between these two animas in Kiefer's soul? In recent works, Kiefer has not repeated the theme of Margarete's golden hair, but his very interesting insistence on Shulamith makes one wonder if Kiefer is playing another of his risky games. For he compulsively repeats the image of the ashen-haired Shulamith who is evidently a shadow anima for the German Anselm Kiefer. Through his obsession with her ashen hair, Kiefer makes Shulamith the center of the Jewish tragedy and of paramount importance to Jewish psychology. Both Celan and Kiefer approach Jewish psychology from the opposite end of the spectrum to that of the inflated collective conception of the "chosen people," a conception that can be seen to block access to a consciousness of the Jewish shadow. The ashen hair of Shulamith, revealing the ethnic biological end of the spectrum, brings a more attuned view to the historical times of "after the catastrophe" in which we are living. For they are times in which there is an upsurge of ethnic conflicts, so much so, that we can say the *Zeitgeist* (spirit of the times) demands an awareness of the deep biological level of the shadow at work in these conflicts.

Kiefer had already included the theme of Shulamith in his masterwork *Zweistromland,* 1985–89, putting her into Book 97. Her presence in this work, makes Shulamith a perennial memory never to be destroyed.

The immense sculpture *Zweistromland/The High Priestess* (pages 74–75), is described by Anne Seymour in the foreword to the book *The High Priestess* as follows:

> The subject of this book is Kiefer's most monumental and ambitious to date. Physically the work consists of two vast steel bookcases, thirteen feet high, standing end to end at a slight angle to one another, like the pages of an open book. Each bookcase

**Zweistromland**
1985–89

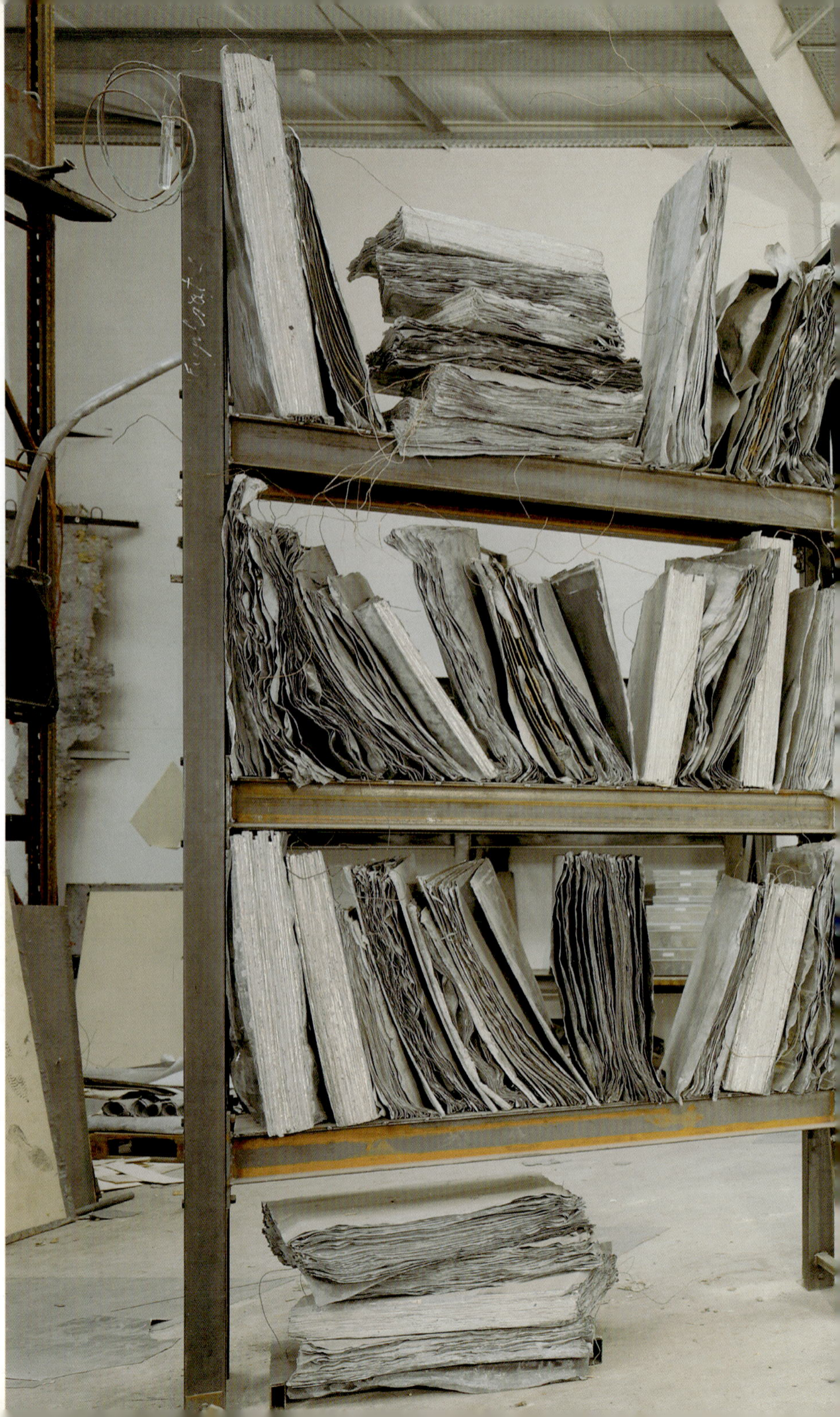

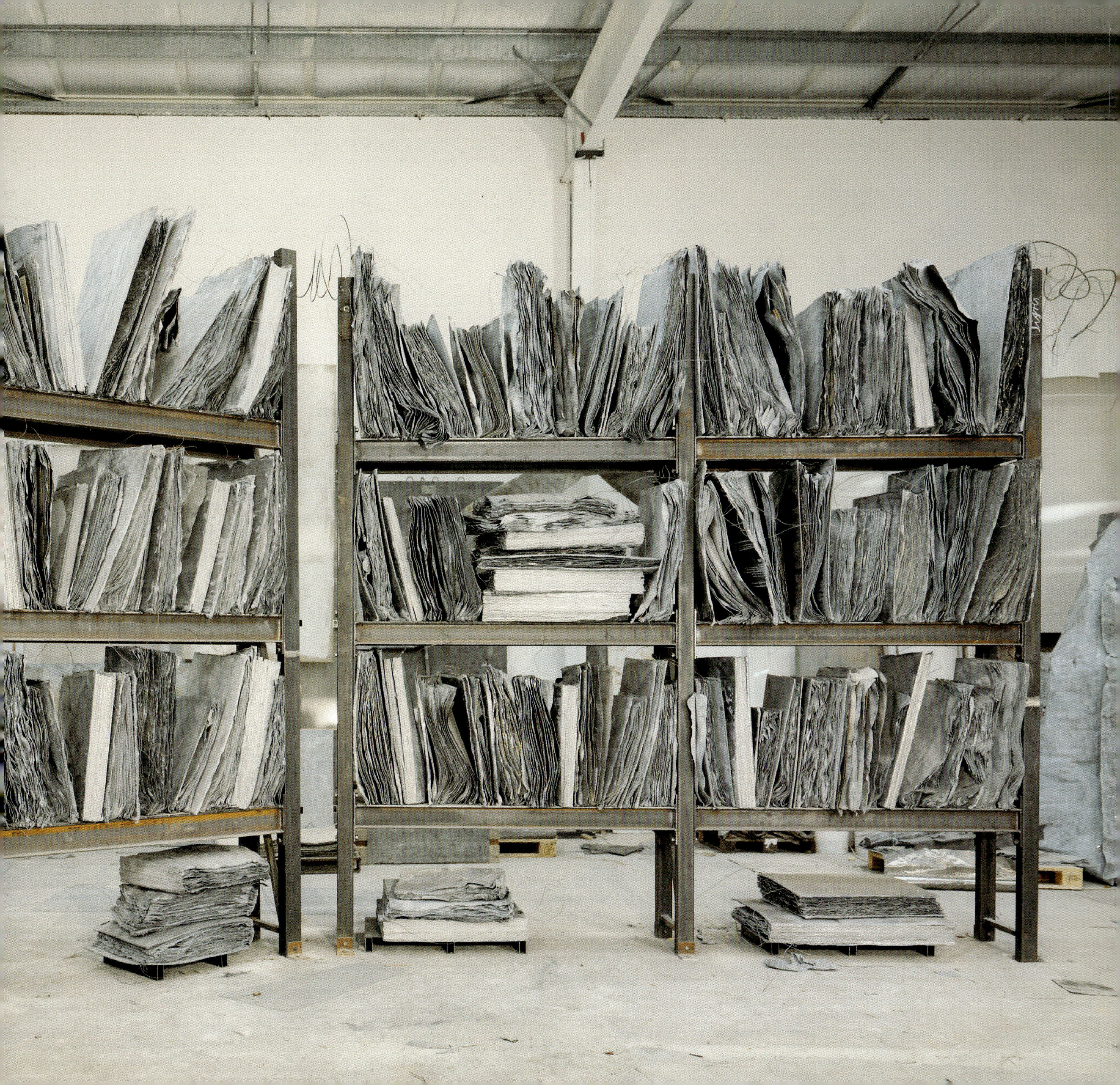

> is filled with massive lead books, some of them empty, some containing images and substances which record the reality of our time (1989: 9).

The library is divided into two parts—Euphrates and Tigris—hence the title *Zweistromland* which means, literally, "two-stream-land," or "land of two rivers," evoking an imagination of the geographical cradle of culture and civilization —Mesopotamia.[12] In his essay, "Observations on a Sculpture by Anselm Kiefer," Armin Zweite writes:

> The title 'Zweistromland' suggests an initially astonishing association of ideas. The allusion is to a civilization whose monuments—unlike those of Egypt, for example—have largely disappeared, and whose settlements have crumbled away: all that remains of the Mesopotamian Empire is a number of unprepossessing mounds of earth in Iraq and Iran (1989: 88).

The quotations above bring a physical description of the sculpture and a historical observation concerning its title. Further to the latter, it seems that Kiefer is concerned with the mystery of the rise and fall of civilizations, bringing to mind the great historians' interest in the mysterious natural forces of creation and destruction. This work activates an uncanny feeling as to how our own civilization is going to end, as has happened to all great civilizations throughout history. Zweite captures this in the image of the "unprepossessing mounds of earth" as all that remains of the great Mesopotamian empire. The sculpture and the imagination it evokes, can be said to produce also an introjection, propitiating reflection upon the mysteries of our own creative and destructive psychological processes.

There is another view of this work, contributed by my friend and colleague, who commented so cogently on the painting *Parsifal:*

> It is a killing weight of book-wisdom in the most base metal: saturnine, catatonic depression at the lowest point of the Solstice. You may imagine the whole bookcase slamming together, fixed like an oyster. It reminds me of the Intolerable Image wherein "time is fixed and space solid." Horrific!

The sculpture is seen as an image of horror, accompanied by a psychiatric vision. With *Parsifal,* Kiefer took a once beautiful and constructive myth and made out of it an image of horror according with the historical reality of today, and now we have *Zweistromland,* another testimony to the times of "after the catastrophe." We can only stand amazed in front of this monumental sculpture, conceived and created out of such a level of depression.

Now let me add my own associations to this work. Kiefer has brought together an imagination of the cradle of civilization with that contained in the alternative title he has given to this work—*The High Priestess.* The high priestess is a figure taken from the second card of the "greater arcana" of the tarot, and it has a strong symbolic meaning. The tradition of the tarot has projected the wisdom of the feminine onto this figure. The high priestess is reproduced in Zweite's essay (1989: 99) and is taken from A. E. Waite's 1909 version of the tarot, in which the figure is conceived within a more esoteric symbolism, undoubtedly influenced by the spiritual theosophical movement and the late nineteenth-century Pre-Raphaelite style. Evidently, with this alternative title, Kiefer's thoughts about the rise and fall of civilizations are intimately related to an image that, besides its esoteric and hermetic complexities, has a Sophia-like quality and compensates Kiefer's flight of ideas. The tarot is a system of divination that functions with archetypal figures within a synchronistic time (see Jung, CW8: 816ff). The two titles of the work suggest that Kiefer has attempted to bring together ideas about the rise and fall of civilizations with the acausal time of the here and now of synchronicity, contained within the image of the high priestess.[13]

Zweite speculates about space and time in his observations (1989: 97), however my approach is to explore it within the limits of the image and in the context of psychology. I see the library as stimulating historical memory, thus freeing and stimulating the imagination, as other works of Kiefer have proved to do. Thus in this powerful work I am reminded of the Alexandrian library that was burned and destroyed by human stupidity under the guise of religious fanaticism in the eighth century. We could propose another association: *Zweistromland* as a mnemonic system. Giulio Camillo's Renaissance Memory Theater was a way of memorizing archetypal images and their correlation at different levels (Yates, 1966: 129 ff), and in *Zweistromland* we can see a memory system in relation to recording the "reality of our time," which in Kiefer's system would be to memorize that which is the most difficult and destructive. Kiefer makes an everlasting memory of the horror and infamy of humankind, in other words, its psychopathic inferiority. We have to keep in mind that the psychopath is unable to remember, he fails to learn to modify his behavior (Kolb, 1983: 496). So there is no experience, merely the automatic repetition of the same stupid behavior. Indeed, I consider this to be the psychological message of *Zweistromland:* to memorize that which by its nature cannot be memorized.

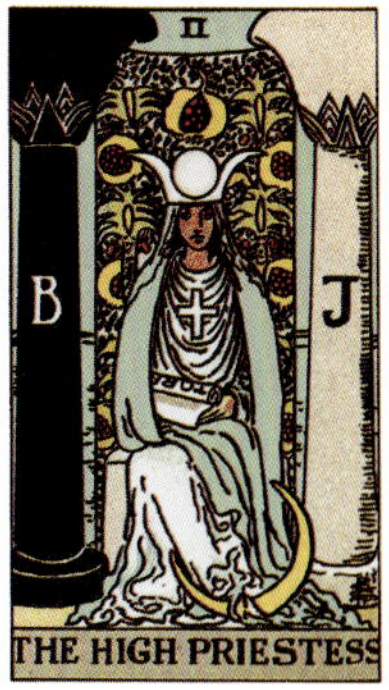

**The High Priestess**

Kiefer made the library when he was in his forties, meaning at an age when he was beginning to move into the second half of life. The paintings that I discuss in this book were done during the first half of life, when he was concerned with reflecting the German collective unconscious and history. With this present work, Kiefer seems to have moved into another level of his psyche and of the collective unconscious. Whatever the psychological state he is expressing with the building of the library, his psyche is archetypally well contained and this, from my point of view, is very important. The forging of the library pertains to the realm of Hephaistos-Wayland,[14] the realm of the master-craftsman, the master of fire and metals, which can hold any psychic condition of the artist.

Let us now try to have a psychological view of Kiefer through two self-portraits he did in 1980, when he was thirty-five, an age at which one begins to reflect about oneself. These self-portraits have the originality of being comprised of photographs that he enriches with attributes of the inner vision he wants to express. The first, *The Starred Heaven,* 1980 (page 80), shows a very opaque photograph of Kiefer in the center of the work. He appears against a painted, black, starry sky. In a misty vision, in a strange solitude, the artist stands on a snake, hands on hip, with his palette, once again the emblem of his individual feelings and art, painted on the site of his heart. The subtitle—*The Starred Heaven Above (us): The Moral Law Within (me)*—is taken from Kant, but I prefer to view this self-portrait from the alchemical notions of the macrocosm and the microcosm. The starry heaven[15] can be equated with the alchemical *scintillae,* the first appearance of the soul. This image brings to mind the alchemist Gerhard Dorn's conception of the *scintillae:*

> Let every man consider diligently in his heart what has been said above, and thus little by little he will come to see with his mental eyes a number of sparks shining day by day and more and more and growing into such a great light that thereafter all things needful to him will be made known (Jung, CW14: 48).

Kiefer's *The Starred Heaven* invites application of the Jungian term, "individuation." Kiefer's sense of moral law has to do with his individuality and is obviously connected to the symbolic site of feeling in the body (the feeling function). The palette painted on his chest, shows the place from which his creative art comes—the heart. I consider Kiefer's art a great achievement in individuation, meaning that he has dealt successfully with unconscious contents of the sort that have most proved to induce identification. The psychological reflections conveyed by Kiefer's work as a whole reveal an unparalleled individuation, one that enables his psyche to withstand the powerful forces of the strong German unconscious.

The second self-portrait, *Broken Flowers and Grass,* 1980 (page 81), complements the first. The two together enable us to form a psychological picture of Kiefer's personality. Kiefer is lying on a bed, eyes closed, dressed in a white-bordered black tunic. The entire forefront of the work is strewn with painted black and white flowers and grass. He looks as if he might be dead. The portrait has a hermetic freakish touch, that of rehearsing one's own death (López-Pedraza, 1989: 187). In Jungian psychotherapy, depression and death have a strong relationship, and their symbolism in dreams is very similar.

Kiefer expressed these complexes in another work: *Resumptio,* 1974 (page 82). It depicts a tomb over which a winged palette hovers. By now, we are well acquainted with the palette as an allegory of Kiefer's creative psyche. In this painting, we see a version of the old imagery of the soul departing from the dead body. This revealing allegory of his soul shows his creativity coming from a tomb. I would say that Kiefer's consciousness functions at a depressive level, and it is from his depression that he is able to produce an art that compensates the impulse of the German collective. Art has its deepest meaning when it compensates the collective consciousness. In this respect, Kiefer has surely proved to be a master.

Returning to the self-portrait *Broken Flowers and Grass,* we see flowers in relation to feeling and depression. For these strange broken flowers would seem to come from the subterranean realm of Persephone, the realm of the dead. Kiefer's feeling function, his depression, and his creativity are bound together indissolubly in his art and individuation.

This self-portrait moves the discussion on depression and creativity onto another level. Kiefer's works convey that his reflections about man's historical tragedy come from a deep depression and, moreover, are reflections that can only be expressed through art. Kiefer demonstrates that he is an artist with the necessary psychic stamina to hold his depression and accept its importance to his nature and creative process. His physique should also be taken into account: he tackles enormous canvases that, besides their creative conception, require a tremendous physical strength.

It seems that most of the alchemical associations I have introduced so far have appeared in Kiefer's paintings spontaneously or organically. But with *Nigredo,* 1984 (page 83), it becomes plain that he has in fact read about alchemy. The title of the painting can only have an alchemical origin. The *nigredo* was the first color the alchemists used to symbolize the alchemical opus.[16] This color was that of the sky just before dawn. The alchemists believed that before the sun begins to rise, the sky is at its darkest. The *nigredo* was called "the darkness, darker than darkness." Jung wrote:

> The *nigredo* or blackness is the initial state, . . . present from the beginning as a quality of the *prima materia,* the chaos or *massa confusa* (CW12: 334).

I see Kiefer as staying in the *nigredo* as an expression of his own nature, promoting a kind of repetition that produces its own psychic movement. From my perspective, *Nigredo* must be seen as an expression of Kiefer's psychological movement downward, toward the earth and its accompanying depression. This painting requires us to stick to the image, and to stay there without considering the other colors of the alchemical process with their redemptive projections.

Kiefer evidently finds his own thread in the alchemical tradition. This concentration on the

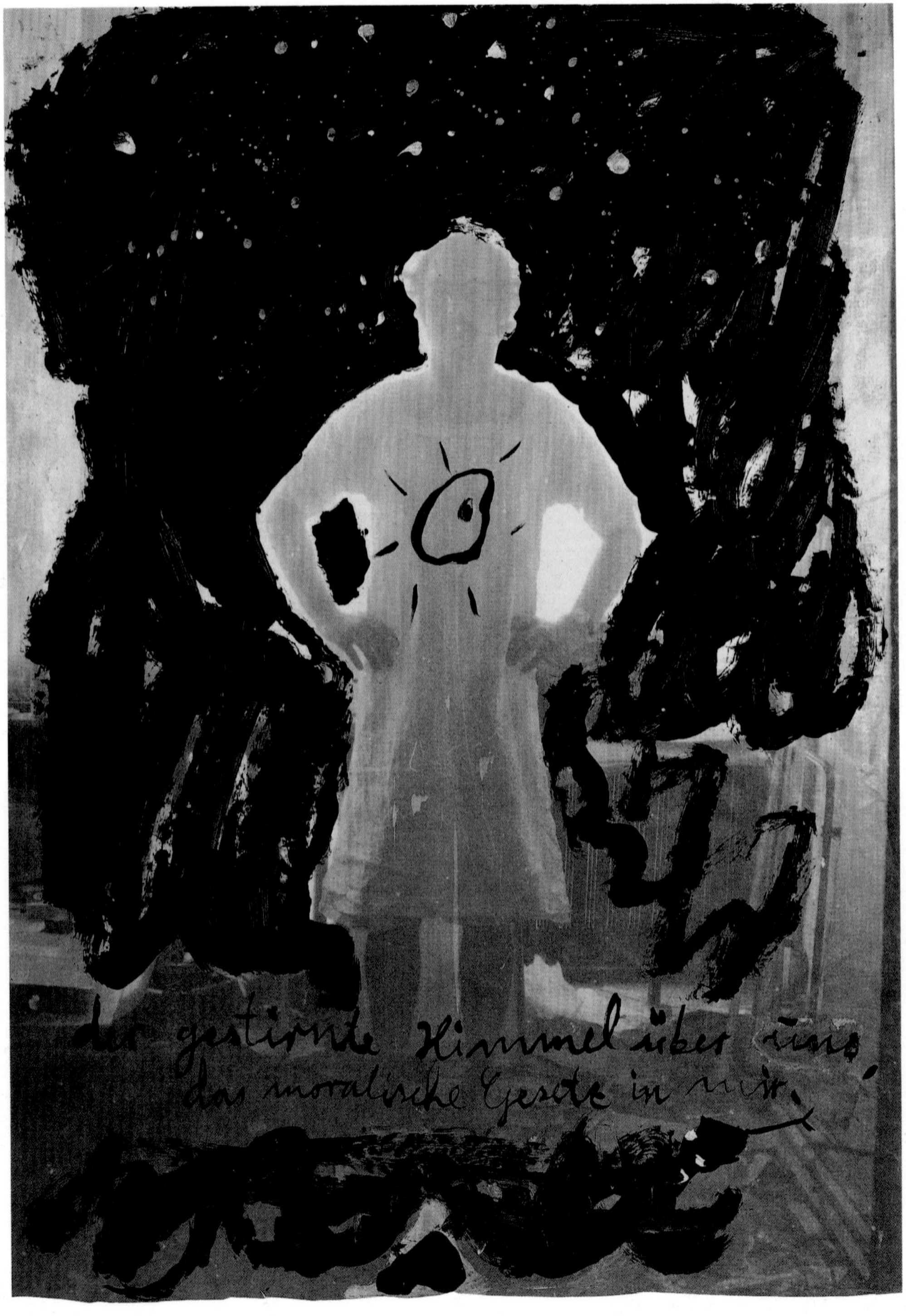


**The Starred Heaven**
1980

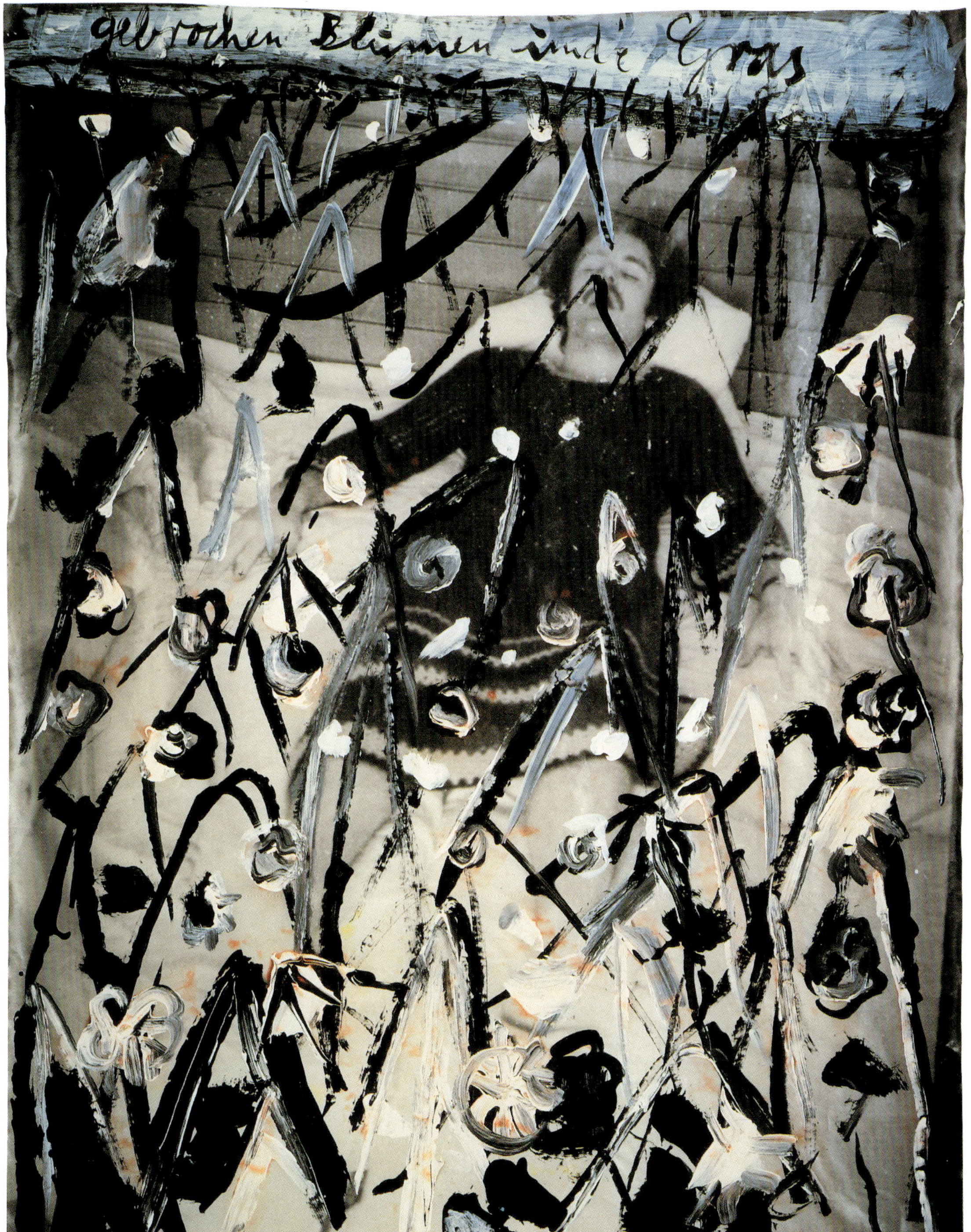


**Broken Flowers and Grass**
1980

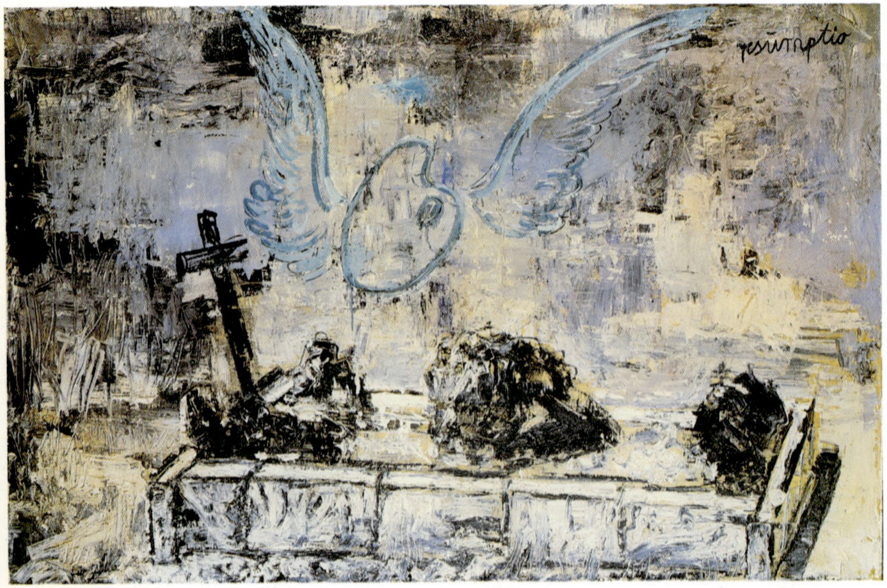


**Resumptio,** 1974

*nigredo* aspect of the alchemical opus, brings to mind those Gnostics who divided the world into three spheres—matter, psyche, and spirit—and concentrated on matter alone (earth equals matter), thinking that by working on this sphere of being, the other two spheres would, indirectly, become apparent. We can translate this to mean that by concentrating on the *nigredo,* psychological and spiritual reflection happen without Kiefer's direct intervention.

Kiefer represents the *nigredo* as plowed earth, furrows stretching to the horizon, with black boulders in the foreground. This links *Nigredo* to Kiefer's use of this imagery, for example in *Siegfried Forgets Brunhilde,* where furrows depict a suffering earth or, to put it another way, as a locus where Kiefer places his suffering and through which he transmits a special emotion. We can speculate also that the furrows convey an image of the alchemical *mortificatio,* which here would mean that which transforms the suffering into psyche and art. The alchemical *mortificatio* had to do with the transformation of the base metals. Through projection upon the process of the metals, a psychological transformation was achieved. Kiefer "mortifies" the earth and through this *mortificatio* his psyche moves.

Kiefer has produced several paintings that can be associated with the emotion of *Nigredo.* One that is especially fascinating in this context is *Cockchafer Fly,* 1974 (page 84). It is an image of the *calcinatio,* the burning of the black earth, which probably corresponds to incineration (see Jung, CW12: 484n.172). The conjunction of earth and fire makes for a hellish vision, one that gives us another view of the alchemical fire so close to Kiefer's artistic creativity. And in *Painting = Burning,* 1974 (page 84), by placing a palette over the tormented, calcified earth, Kiefer verifies the extent to which his art stems from such psychological levels. This all would suggest that his emotional impact resides in the painting of such powerful images.

Although alchemy may have appeared in Kiefer's work via the unconscious, it is safe to say that now he has a direct interest in associating with this very rich tradition. He also connects directly to the German history of art as a follower

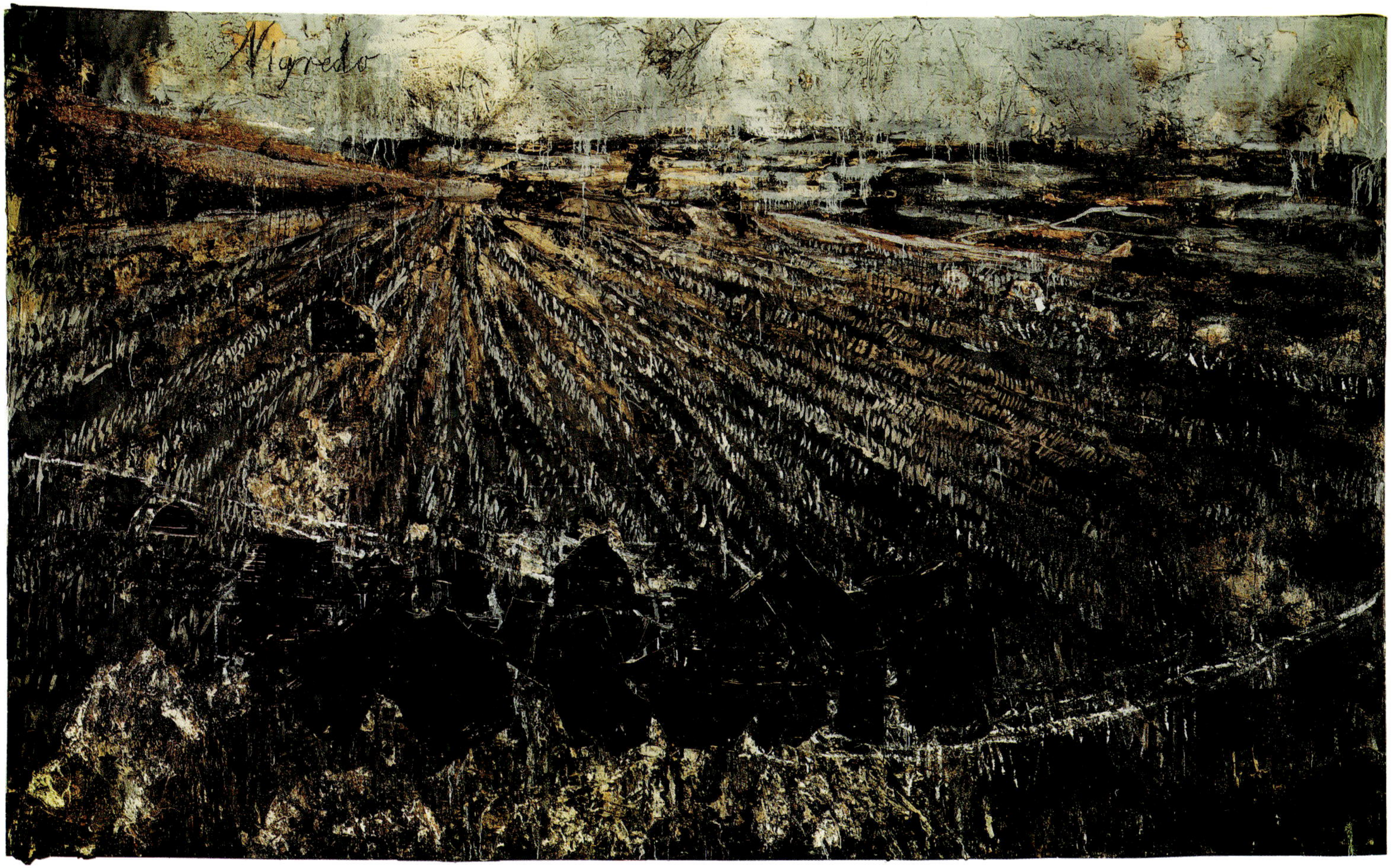


**Nigredo,** 1984

of Dürer, especially through the latter's famous *Melancholia*.[17] It is in alchemy and Dürer's art that Kiefer has most likely found two German traditions that have preserved individual values. Perhaps he senses that his own nature is protected within these traditions.

Peter-Klaus Schuster (1991), among other art critics, has commented on Kiefer and melancholia in the catalogue to the exhibition *Saturne en Europe,* 1991, to which Kiefer contributed seventeen pictures and nine books, among which was a painting called *Melancholia*. Schuster offers a summary of the relation between melancholia and the creation of art in the Western culture.[18] His essay describes the background to the tradition that Kiefer follows, namely, that art and melancholy go together.[19] Schuster (1991: 156) brings an image that I see as an allegory of Kiefer's creative nature: he describes a painting within a painting by Adam Elsheimer (1578–1648) in which there is a naked genius of the arts in the top part, striving to reach heaven with a winged hand. His flight is hampered by a naked satyr and an old man on crutches who are tying a stone to his leg. In the upward striving of the genius of the arts one sees the mercurial flight of the *puer aeternus*, but this flight is compensated by two very depressive forces in human nature: the naked satyr personifying the Dionysian, primitive, theatrical, down-to-earth side of depression and the old man on crutches, personifying the saturnine side, with its physical afflictions and limitations. They represent two basic sides of depression, two different ways into the downward pull of the body. These two compensatory archetypal forces, the moist satyr and the dry Saturn, in a tension with the upward flight of the *puer,* seem to be dominant forces in Kiefer. Kiefer's art reminds us of the importance of the psychology of this combination of two archetypes that have been so repressed by the ruling consciousness of Western cul-

**Cockchafer Fly**
1974

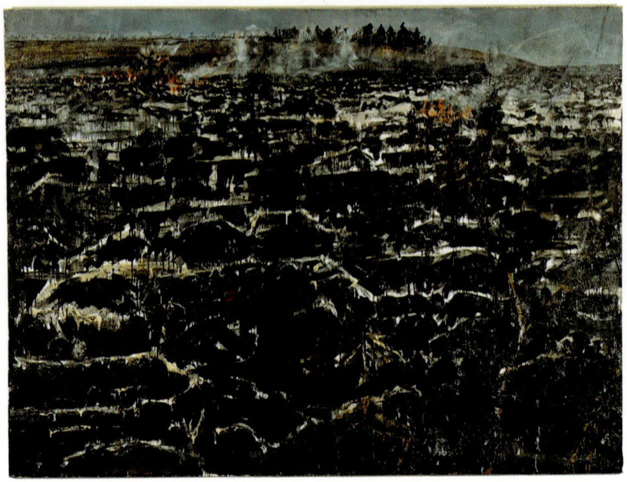

**Painting = Burning**
1974

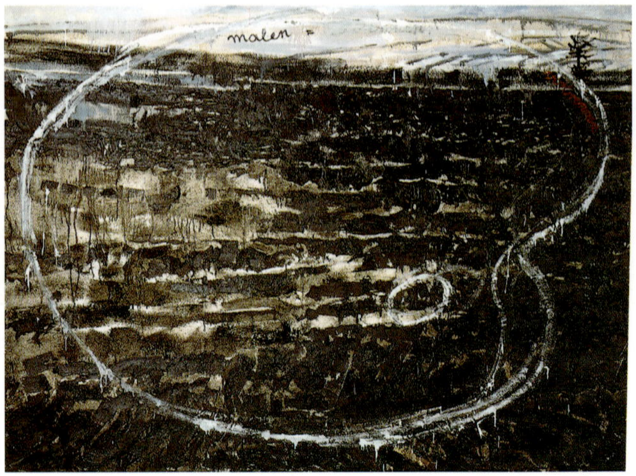

ture. It is exemplified in a sculpture, *Palette with Wings,* 1985–86 (page 86), in which the winged ascensional aspect of the creative palette is compensated by the heavy metals of lead and steel, of which it is made. The wings, representing flying adolescent psychology, look too heavy to fly.

Following this line, Schuster quotes from Kiefer's introduction to a recent Berlin exhibition in which Kiefer shows just how aware he is that these two archetypal bodily forces are the sources of his art:

> I am opposed to the genius idea. It applied to a specific period. The idea that by means of genius you can create something out of nothing was held for a very short time during the nineteenth century. . . . In my own experience the most important ideas come to me when I am doing something quite ordinary, when I am doing stupid odds and ends like cleaning up a table. While repairing an old leaden water pipe, I had the idea of lead engraving. It is not the grandiose but the banal things that generate future developments (1991: 158).

Kiefer's description of thc way his creative ideas come to him through cleaning a table or mending an old lead pipe, is akin to a psychotherapeutic approach. It is while he is doing "stupid odds and ends," doing banal ordinary things that an *abaissement du niveau mental,* a lowering of consciousness, happens. This lowered consciousness allows for a connection to the archetypal forces gathered in the unconscious, propitiating psychic movement. Here Kiefer is giving us a simple and practical lesson in psychology.

I would like the reader to take this latter part of the book, where I touch on Kiefer's psychology more directly, as a background for approaching *Saturn Time,* 1986 (page 88). In this painting Kiefer renders a connection to his saturnine complex in beautiful, deep strange blues, with ferns and lead. The lungs, painted at the base of the fern, like the heart allegorized by the palette in *The Starred Heaven,* can also be seen as an allegory, this time for life on earth. The heart and the lungs complement each other and are both in the part of the body above the diaphragm. In the kundalini yoga, the *Anajata chakra,* situated above the diaphragm in the chest, is the place of feeling. One of the jewels in Jung's legacy is his 1932 seminars on the kundalini yoga,[20] where he demonstrates that the Hindu tantric system of the *chakras,* when taken symbolically and with some corrections and modifications, is also valid for Western man. Taking the *chakras* as centers of consciousness in the body, Jung tried to "rescue" that which has been the most repressed in Western culture, namely, the psychology of the body.[21] I have already noted the connection between Kiefer's feelings and his creative depression and, here, the lungs could be seen as representing a feeling relation to the time of Saturn, which would be equal to a Saturnian

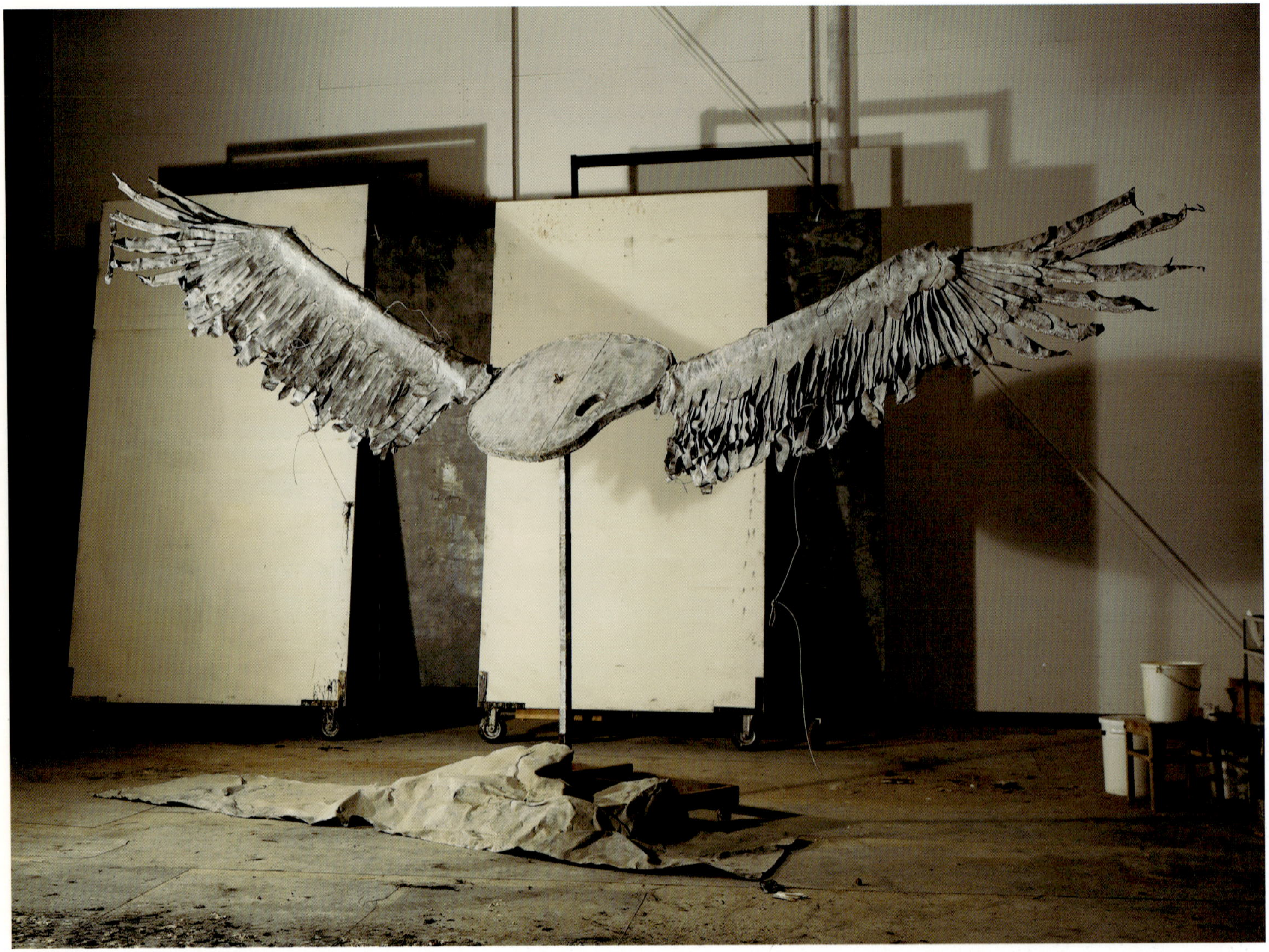

**Palette With Wings,** 1985–86

consciousness. This could be another association to Kiefer's own saturnine nature and the feeling value he gives to it.

Through alchemy, we saw a psychosomatic connection in *Father, Son, Holy Ghost* and now, in *Saturn Time,* a psychosomatic connection—with different complexities—can also be made to the lungs. It is worth noting how breathing is immediately affected by emotions and physical effort, and how this can give access to a consciousness of feeling and body. Jung was very aware of the ascensional psychic movement in Western civilization, achieved at the expense of the emotional body through millennia of repression.[22] Jungian psychotherapy is a process based on the downward movement of the psyche toward the body and the difficult task of trying to make conscious psychosomatic processes and illnesses. Kiefer's work is revealing in this context, because, as we have identified, his paintings contain a compensatory downward movement. With *Saturn Time,* for example, we can move further in this direction and see that saturnine consciousness and time is also the time of a psychotherapy whose concern is to propitiate an incubation that modifies the time and timing of the psyche, thus aiding a connection to the repressed emotional body.

One of Jung's most innovative ideas was to find the relation between the instincts and the archetypes. This opened the way to an exploration of deeper levels of human nature, that is to say, to an exploration in more biological terms. We began this book with Jung's use of the term "biology" in relation to Wotan, understanding it, metaphorically, as a way to see through and into the strange behavior of the German people, in other words, as a way to see through and into a shadow which, because we have no image of it, can only be accepted at that biological level as the shadow per se.

Rosenthal brings another association to *Saturn Time* by way of an interview with Kiefer:

> The fern has existed almost since the beginning of the physical world, according to the artist. The fern forest is associated with a period preceding the ice age, and from the fern came early forms of energy, including coal and wood (1987: 153).

This allows us to view the painting as a way to imagine the time of evolution, implicit in the title *Saturn Time.* There is no other way to imagine the time of evolution than from a consciousness that pertains to it; in other words, from an archetypal saturnine consciousness.

We have to appreciate that, in our attempts to gain a consciousness of evolution, the knowledge we can gather from archetypes, instincts and biology, while valuable, is at best only "superficial notions" (to borrow the words of the poet) brought to what is an unknowable immensity. The superficiality of our notions about evolution cannot be stressed enough. As we have seen,

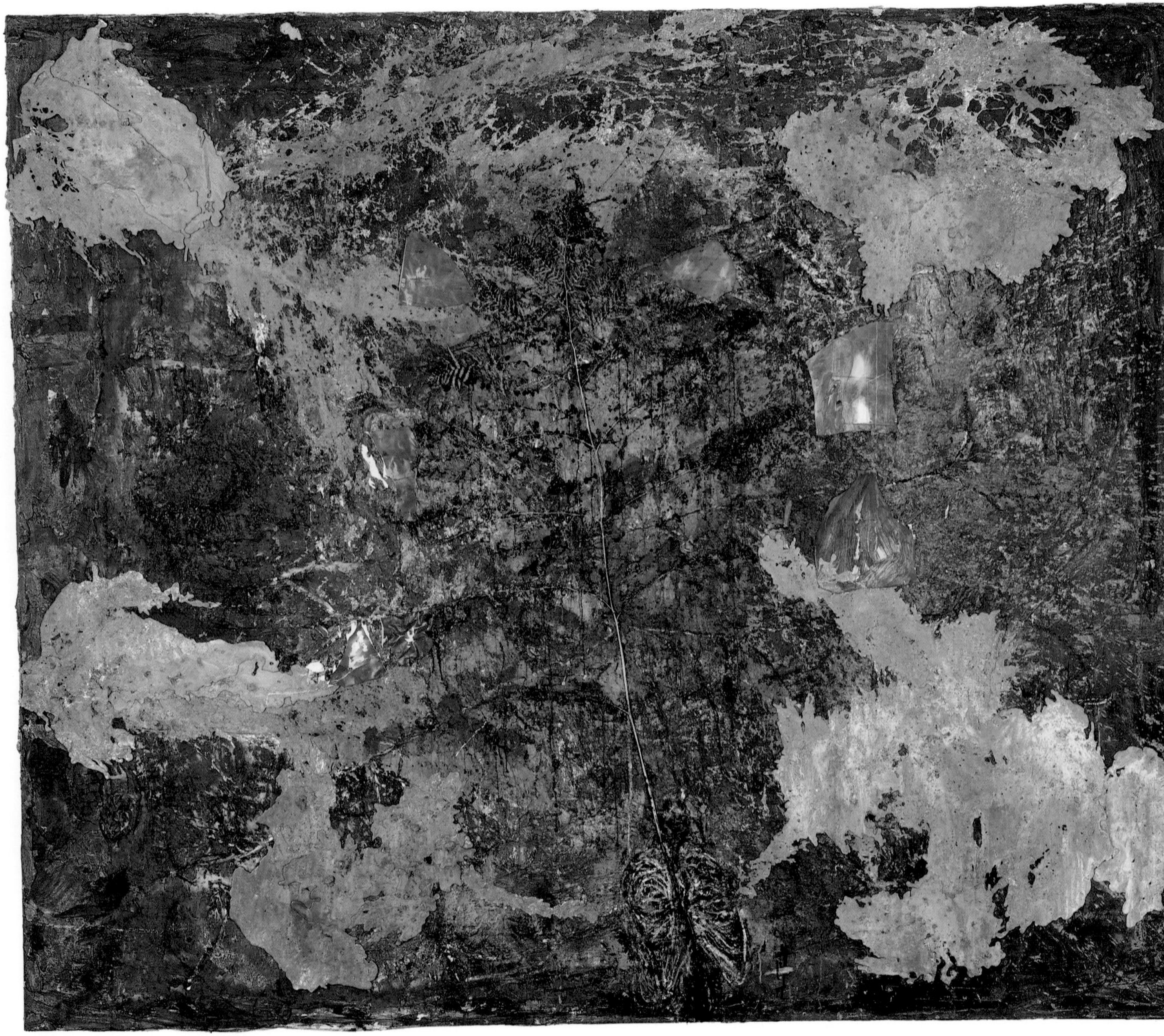

**Saturn Time,** 1986

Kiefer has made out of the visual arts an instrument of reflection, such as in *Saturn Time,* where his associations with evolution offer a different perspective on the historical and religious themes I have discussed in regard to his work.

In connecting to Saturn, the god upon whom the ascensional dominant consciousness of Western culture has projected a most pernicious influence, Kiefer brings to mind the alchemists and Renaissance philosophers who worshiped and propitiated Saturn. Kiefer offers an up-to-date lesson: to be in close contact with that which, when repressed, can have a destructive effect and poison the soul. As old Cronus, Saturn is the god who has always ruled time. Now, after ruminating over Kiefer's painting, we can imagine Saturn rules the consciousness of the time of evolution, which is close to the mysterious forces of creation and destruction, a consciousness wherein these two opposites are not split in the way they have been throughout history. Undoubtedly, saturnine consciousness could be seen as the consciousness pertaining to the times of "after the catastrophe."

At the four corners of the painting are spots of beautiful lead and a fern at its center, making a mandala, which creates an inner Saturnian space from which to meditate upon the origins of life on earth. Lastly, this painting has a strong religious feeling to it. If we think about, or meditate on, the immensity of evolution, it gives us a religious feeling that cannot be excluded from today's consciousness.

There are many insights into psychology that are to be gained through study of Anselm Kiefer's rich body of art. Kiefer's work touches a psychological place where the psyche is moved deeply. His work encourages this psychological exploration, and rewards the viewer who approaches it from the discipline of psychology, as well as from the history of art and ideas.

# Notes

Passages from *The Collected Works of C. G. Jung* are referred to in the text by volume and paragraph number. Other books are referenced in the text and notes by page numbers.

1. For a clear definition of the shadow see *A Critical Dictionary of Jungian Analysis*, eds. Andrew Samuels, B. Shorter, and F. Plaut, (Routledge and Kegan Paul: London, 1986), where it says:

   > In 1945 Jung gave a most direct and clear-cut definition of the shadow: 'the thing a person has no wish to be' (CW16: 470). In this simple statement is subsumed the many-sided and repeated references to shadow as the negative side of the personality, the sum of all the unpleasant qualities one wants to hide, the inferior, worthless and primitive side of man's nature, the 'other person' in one, one's own dark side (p. 138).

2. There are many examples of this sort of regression in the history of art. Two artists come to mind: Paul Gauguin, who went to Tahiti, where he made great art out of his contact with primitive man and his myths, and Pablo Picasso, who went to Gosol, where he took a step backward into his Iberian Mediterranean roots before making the leap forward into *Les Demoiselles d'Avignon*, a painting that changed the visual arts forever.
3. One senses that psychology has been unable to reflect its own stupidity, which frequently appears in theoretical and therapeutical "strategies," reminding one of *Operation Sea Lion I.*
4. The Iconoclastic Controversy, a dispute over the use of religious images (icons) in the Byzantine Empire during the eighth and ninth centuries. The Iconoclasts (those who rejected images) objected to icon worship for several reasons, including the Old Testament prohibition against images in the Ten Commandments (Ex. 20: 4) and the possibility of idolatry. The defender of icon worship insist-

ed on the symbolic nature of images and on the dignity of created matter (*Enc. Brit.*, 1980. V: 283).

5. Picasso made a rather similar process of abstraction with the image of the bull, but in his case, the process transmits an experimental attitude very different to the fanatical attitude one sees in Mondrian.
6. This alchemical imagination fits with the information as to the purpose of his trip given by Theodore Stebbins and Susan Cragg Ricci (1988).
7. "For the Master of Bayreuth was not only Hitler's greatest exemplar; he was also the young man's ideological mentor" (Fest, 1975: 56).
8. This victory checked the emperor Augustus' plans for the country between the Rhine and Elbe rivers. Later, in a battle with Germanicus Caesar, Arminius' wife, Thusnelda, was captured. In A.D. 16, Arminius survived a full-scale Roman attack. He was eventually murdered by his own people. In the nineteenth century, he was glorified as a German national hero, backed by Tacitus' judgement of him as "unquestionably the liberator of Germany" (*Enc. Brit.*, 1980, I: 527).
9. In the dream seminars, Jung was making a comparison to Jewish psychology, where consciousness is "strong" and the unconscious "weak," meaning that most of the psychological energy is in consciousness. See also CW10: 353–54.
10. Kiefer's depiction of Shulamite would seem to have an affinity to the psychological confusion of well-known Jewish scholar and literary critic Theodor Adorno over the possibility of writing poetry after the Holocaust: "After Auschwitz to write poetry is barbaric." Later, it seems he changed his mind:

    > Perennial suffering has as much right to expression as a tortured man has to scream; hence it may have been wrong to say that after Auschwitz you could no longer write poems (Colin, 1991: xvii).

11. This short biographical note on Paul Celan has been taken from the "Nota Biográfica" by Jesús Munárriz, in Paul Celan's *Amapola y Memoria,* who in turn took it from Israel Chaften's *Paul Celan: Eine Biographie seiner Jugend* (Frankfurt am Main; Insel Verlag, 1979). I have also referred to Colin (1991).
12. I shall use the title *Zweistromland* as Zweite uses it in his commentary in the book *The High Priestess.* But the reader might keep in mind that it can be translated as Mesopotamia.
13. For an interpretation of the tarot from the perspective of Jungian psychology, see Nichols (1980).
14. Wayland is the Nordic mythic counterpart to the Greek Hephaistos, the master craftsman.
15. The starry heaven also brings to mind van Gogh's *The Starry Night* (1889).
16. The other colors of the alchemical process were the *albedo* (white) and *rubedo* (red), the sequence of the colors at dawn.
17. For a discussion of Albrecht Dürer's *Melancholia,* see Erwin Panofsky, *The Life and Art of Albrecht Dürer* (Princeton Univ. Press: Princeton, 1971), pp. 157–71.
18. Schuster refers to the classical and Renaissance

authors Aristotle and Ficino, and medieval astronomers and alchemists to back his approach, as well as to the scholars of the Warburg Institute in London–Panofsky, Saxl, and Klibansky–who have studied Dürer's *Melancholia* in *Saturn and Melancholy* (Thomas Nelson & Sons, Ltd.: London, 1964); see also Walter Benjamin, *The Origin of the German Drama*, trans. John Osborne (NLB: London, 1977).

19. I give full recognition to the writers and critics who have discussed Kiefer's melancholy. Melancholy comes from the classical theory of the humors that was taken up in medieval times. I, however, prefer to use the term depression, because it has less romantic associations, and to combine it with an archetypal approach rather than that of the humors.
20. These seminars were to discuss a series of lectures on the kundalini yoga given by Professor Wilhelm Hauer in Zurich, in the same year.
21. See Onians (1973: 25ff), where he discusses the heart and lungs as organs of consciousness connected to emotion.
22. See Stanford (1983: 5), where he mentions the early process of repression of the emotions, which means also the repression of the consciousness of the body. It is a process that continues in the Westerner who thinks about the body only scientifically and physically, not psychically.

# Bibliography


Adriani, Götz. 1991. *The Books of Anselm Kiefer 1969–1990.* Trans. Bruni Mayor. New York: George Braziller, Inc. London: Thames and Hudson.

Celan, Paul. 1980. *Poems.* Trans. Michael Hamburger. New York: Persea Books.

—— 1985. *Amapola y Memoria.* Trans. Jesús Munárriz. Madrid: Ediciones Hiperión.

Colin, Amy. 1991. *Paul Celan: Holograms of Darkness.* Bloomington and Indianapolis: Indiana University Press.

Donnington, Robert. 1963. *Wagner's 'Ring' and its Symbols: The Music and the Myth.* London: Faber and Faber.

Fest, Joachim. 1975. *Hitler.* Trans. Richard and Clara Winston. New York: Vintage Books.

Jung, Carl Gustav. 1953– *The Collected Works.* Vols. 1–20. Trans. R. F. C. Hull. Eds. Sir Herbert Read, M. Fordham, G. Adler, and W. McGuire. Princeton: Princeton University Press, and London: Routledge and Kegan Paul. They are cited below by volume number and title.

—— 1953. CW12: *Psychology and Alchemy.*

—— 1956. CW5: *Symbols of Transformation.*

—— 1959. CW9ii: *Aion: Researches into the Phenomenology of the Self.*

—— 1960. CW8: *The Structure and Dynamics of the Psyche.*

—— 1964. CW10: *Civilization in Transition.*

—— 1967. CW13: *Alchemical Studies.*

—— 1963. *Memories, Dreams, Reflections.* Ed. Aniela Jaffé. London: Collins and Routledge and Kegan Paul.

Jung, Emma and Marie-Louise von Franz. 1971. *The Grail Legend.* Trans. Andrea Dykes. London: Hodder & Stoughton.

Kolb, Lawrence C. 1973. *Modern Clinical Psychiatry.* Philadelphia: W. B. Saunders Company.

López-Pedraza, Rafael. 1989. *Hermes and His Children*. Einsiedeln: Daimon Verlag.

—— 1990. *Cultural Anxiety*. Einsiedeln: Daimon Verlag.

Munárriz, Jesús. 1985. "Nota Biográfica." In Celan, 1985.

Nichols, Sallie. 1980. *Jung and Tarot: An Archetypal Journey*. York Beach, Maine: Samuel Weisser.

Onians, Richard Broxton. 1973. *The Origins of European Thought*. New York: Arno Press.

Rosenthal, Mark. 1987. *Anselm Kiefer*. Chicago: The Art Institute of Chicago, and Philadelphia: The Philadelphia Museum of Art.

Scholem, Gershom. 1965. *On the Kabbalah and Its Symbolism*. Trans. Ralph Manheim. New York: Schocken Books.

Schuster, Peter-Klaus. 1991. *Anselm Kiefer 10 Marz-Mai 1991*. Berlin: Staatliche Museen, Preussischer Kulturbesitz.

Seymour, Anne. 1989. "Foreword." In Zweite, 1989.

Stanford, William Bedell. 1983. *Greek Tragedy and the Emotions*. London: Routledge and Kegan Paul.

Stebbins, Jr., Theodore E. and Susan Cragg Ricci. 1988. *A Book by Anselm Kiefer*. New York: George Braziller, Inc., and Boston: Museum of Fine Arts, Boston.

*The Encyclopaedia Britannica*. 1980. Ed. Philip W. Goetz. Chicago: Chicago University Press.

Toynbee, Arnold. 1946. *A Study of History*. Vols. I–VI. Abridged by D. C. Somervell. London: Oxford University Press.

—— 1979. *A Study of History*. Revised and abridged by the author and Jane Caplan. New York: Weathervane Books.

Yates, Frances A. 1966. *The Art of Memory*. London: Routledge & Kegan Paul.

Ziegler, Alfred. 1983. *Archetypal Medicine*. Trans. Gary V. Hartman. Dallas: Spring Publications

Zweite, Armin. 1989. *The High Priestess*. London: Anthony d'Offay Gallery, and Thames and Hudson.

# List of Illustrations





For those readers interested in a full description of the materials used by Anselm Kiefer for his paintings, sculptures, photographs, and books, see: *Anselm Kiefer,* 1987 (catalogue) by Mark Rosenthal; *The Books of Anselm Kiefer 1969–1990* by Götz Adriani, which includes facsimiles of *Heroic Symbols,* 1969; *To Genet,* 1969; *Operation Sea Lion,* 1975; *Iconoclastic Controversy II,* 1980; *Shulamith,* 1990; and *Shulamith,* 1990; *A Book by Anselm Kiefer* by Theodore E. Stebbins, Jr. and Susan Cragg Ricci, a facsimile of *Erotik im Fernen Osten oder: Transition from cool to warm,* 1988; and *The High Priestess* by Armin Zweite. Editorial data on these books may be found in the Bibliography. For a complete listing of Anselm Kiefer's books, please refer to *The Books of Anselm Kiefer 1969–1990.*